O U G H T E N
H O U S E
P U B L I C A T I O N S

"Books and Tools for the Rising Planetary Consciousness"

JEWELS ON THE PATH

TRANSFORMATIONAL TEACHINGS OF THE ASCENDED MASTERS

BY

ERIC KLEIN

Editing & Typography by Sara Benjamin-Rhodes
Cover Illustration by Cathie Beach
Published by Oughten House Publications
Livermore, California USA

JEWELS ON THE PATH

TRANSFORMATIONAL TEACHINGS OF THE ASCENDED MASTERS

COVER ILLUSTRATION BY CATHIE BEACH
EDITING & TYPOGRAPHY BY SARA BENJAMIN-RHODES

PUBLISHED BY:
OUGHTEN HOUSE PUBLICATIONS
P.O. BOX 2008
LIVERMORE, CALIFORNIA, 94551-2008 USA

Library of Congress Cataloging-in-Publication Data
Jewels on the path : transformational teachings of the Ascended
Masters / by Eric Klein.
            p.   cm.
    ISBN 1-880666-48-0 (alk. paper): $14.95
    1. Spirit writings.   2. Ascended masters.   3. Spiritual life--
Miscellanea.   I. Klein, Eric, 1951-
BF1290.J48   1995
133.9'3--dc20   95-35050
                                                    CIP

ISBN 1-880666-48-0, Trade Publication

iv

TABLE OF CONTENTS

(continued)

TABLE OF CONTENTS (CONT.)

THE IMPORTANCE OF DISCERNMENT

In editing a book for Oughten House, I strive to take it to the highest level of which I am capable. I draw upon my intuition and experience and try to catch anything that is not accurate or clear. However, there are as many pictures of reality as there are points of awareness to formulate them. There are many destiny patterns unfolding simultaneously. We each need to use our own discernment to distinguish what is "ours" and what is someone else's. No source of information is without its distortion. Even the clearest channels are not, nor have they ever been, 100% accurate. Even within information that is "mostly true," there is some information that is not true. Even within information that is "mostly false," there is some truth present.

Your greatest ally in finding your way to your own "destination" is your own discernment. No one can know your own answers except you. You cannot rely on anyone or anything outside of you: your answers all lie within you. We are all unique aspects of the One. There is no duplication whatsoever, which is pretty amazing in itself. As you read what is in these pages, take what is "yours" and embrace it. The rest may be there for someone else. If it helps you on your path, then it has served.

— Sara Benjamin-Rhodes, Managing Editor

PUBLISHER'S NOTE

The channeled material presented in this book, *Jewels on the Path*, is a form of documentary concerning spiritual matters. It consists of transmitted information. The reader's interpretation of this or any other channeled information is strictly subjective and reflects his or her personal beliefs.

The language used in this book has been transcribed with the intention of presenting the actual transmissions of the Masters, with the least possible alteration in meaning. Because of this, there are a few words used in unconventional ways. The essence of the material remains unchanged.

We at Oughten House extend our wholehearted appreciation and gratitude to each of our Literary Producers for making this publication possible: Marge and John Melanson, Barbara Rawles, Robin Drew, Irit Levy, Debbie Detwiler, Kiyo Monro, Alice Tang, Eugene P. Tang, Brad Clarke, Victor Beasley, Ruth Dutra, Nicole Christine, Dennis Donahue, Fred J. Tremblay, Kathy Cook, Debbie Soucek, and Kimberley Mullen.

DEDICATED

To all living Masters: your presence here saves the world.

To sincere aspirants of all persuasions: your open hearts illuminate the path for all who will follow.

To my dear Praty: for helping me across the crystal bridge.

ACKNOWLEDGMENTS

To Jenny Annear and Marie Damschen for endless transcription. To Sara Benjamin-Rhodes for her wonderful editing assistance and typography. To the staff at Oughten House for all your efforts. To Christine for her undying love and support.

Jewels on the Path ⟞

PREFACE

Looking back over the channeled teachings that are the foundation of this and my previous books, I am impressed by the gentle yet powerful ways the Masters have gradually opened us to new depths of experience. It seems we receive just the teaching, just the intensity of spiritual presence, we are capable of integrating in each session. None of us who are sharing in this adventure (which many Westerners have labeled the "ascension path") can deny the love and care that have been showered upon us in our often feeble attempts to experience and to describe what ascension is and what it means. I have walked this path for many years, only to find I am ultimately reduced to a state of wonder.

I believe there are many others on the spiritual path who are experiencing these same wonderful, yet challenging, transformations. It is for you I have prepared these channelings, these "Jewels on the Path." Those who require and remain fascinated by the grosser manifestations of the planetary ascension process (prophecies and predictions, Earth changes, alien encounters, etc.) may wish to look elsewhere for their sustenance. But for those who, like myself, are becoming less interested in the obvious physical evidence of change, even as the need for *real* spiritual food is growing, the contents of these pages will feed you well.

The essence of truth, the God presence, exists throughout every dimension in innumerable changing forms through all space and time. The purpose of any spiritual path, whatever language or belief systems are used to describe it, is to facilitate a practical realization of this ultimate truth. This attainment, often referred to as enlightenment, self-realization, or God-realization, results in a permanent and effortless awareness of our union with the Divine in each moment, independent of ongoing situations, thoughts, and emotions. To paraphrase the Buddha, the experience of a personal identity separate from God is the fundamental illusion that creates all suffering, here on Earth or anywhere else it exists. The realization of our ultimate "oneness" with God is both the source of human peace and our ticket to true liberation. The breakthrough to this cosmic awareness is what transforms a student into a master. All of the teachers speaking to us in these channelings achieved this state of God-realization prior to their attainment of the ascended state, and their teachings here indicate it will be the same for us. Many times in recent years I have heard them say, "The path to the doorway of ascension passes through the corridor of self-realization."

The sublime paradox is that once this realization is achieved (the complete manifestation — not merely the various experiential steps and stages, of which there are many), a being no longer has a burning desire to escape the apparent limitations of the physical body via the ascension, for all forms and all dimensional manifestations are seen to be equally illusory! From that point on there is only oneness, bliss, and selfless surrender to the needs of the moment in spontaneous service to the divine will.

I have been blessed to have sat at the feet of physical masters (God-realized teachers) and these attributes have applied to each of them, no matter which spiritual path they traveled to reach enlightenment. I have also been shown the way spiritual teachers are held karmically accountable for their actions on Earth. I have seen the purity required to radiate that light in this world, and the total surrender necessary to be a real servant of divine love in this realm of shadowy reflections, partial truth, and resistance. I have seen many, in recent years, attempting to reap the rewards of the true teacher without first passing through the purifications that enable one to reach that inspired state. This may be a valuable lesson for them, but there is no need for you to partake of unripe fruit when there are real Masters, physical and invisible, working among us. Seek and you *will* find!

I encourage all who wish to fully enjoy the feast of Spirit, in whatever way, from whatever path, to hold fast to the honest expression of that simplicity and humility which are the prerequisites to self-mastery, God-realization, and ascension. Know that spiritual truth cannot be understood or explained by the mind. It can only be known by direct personal experience. Know that all beliefs and teachings must ultimately be abandoned at the gate, for only the pure of heart can enter there. Here are some of the invisible stores you will need to complete the journey.

— Eric Klein
Santa Cruz, California
July 1995

Jewels on the Path ≋

INTRODUCTION
by Sananda

Life is an ever-expanding spiral of growth and experience. It carries us through many forms and many realms of existence, all of which are sacred. For you whose spirits now inhabit the human form on this planet Earth, an opportunity exists to take a quantum leap in your development, in the conscious awareness of who you are in the unfolding divine drama. In order to take full advantage of this opportunity, you require assistance in the form of teaching, and through the sharing of what I will simply refer to as "transformational interactions."

The purest form of teaching involves the sharing of information that can guide the student to their own unique experience of the subject matter, without creating limiting conceptual barriers that must be transcended at a later stage of the path. This is a delicate and challenging task, especially so when the subject matter is itself spiritual. With the cooperation of this dedicated channel we have done our utmost to transmit information that will serve humanity at this critical time. More can always be said, but the essential understandings that have been presented here and in the previous books, *The Crystal Stair* and *The Inner Door*, will provide necessary and fundamental guidance to those awakening to the reality of the planetary ascension process.

Once the basic information has been shared and understood, the real work of integration begins. This is where the transformational aspect takes over, pulling the student beyond the realms of the mind into real spiritual growth. It is this stage of the path that separates the dedicated truth-seeker from the merely curious, and many decide at this point to postpone these more difficult growth processes until some later time.

The "transformational interactions" that occur during this later stage of the path are energetic teachings, transmitted from spirit to spirit, far beyond the level of language. It becomes the role of the student to simply learn to open and receive these loving and healing energies. The channelings in this collection can be truly magical in this regard, depending upon the openness and sensitivity of the reader.

Trust that we are with you. Trust that we are doing all we can to lift you beyond sorrow into the deepest experience of love, the real essence of who you are. Know that the path is challenging, but also know that the rewards are indescribable. Open and receive your passport to conscious immortality.

CHAPTER ONE

COSMIC RADIO

❧ Sananda ❧

Hello, my dear friends. It's good to be with you this day. This is Sananda with you. I thank you for your time and energy. I thank you for allowing our worlds to intersect in this moment. There is much that we can accomplish together this day. You see, I am here on a business trip. I am in the business of transformation, and you are my clientele. Today we will share some very healing energies. There are many Masters of love and light surrounding this gathering. We will be speaking to you through this channel, as a group, while we are working individually with each of you to whatever degree you are capable of absorbing our energies. This is dependent upon your openness, your willingness to relax and surrender to the transformation that is occurring.

We have been very active lately in my business: Ascended Masters, Incorporated. We have affiliates in the Ashtar Command and the angelic multitudes, as well. We are working very intensely now with you, through you — and sometimes in spite of you! — to assist the transformation that is occurring on this world.

There is a great ray, a great force of light and love, beaming, surrounding, entering this world. This energy has always been present, as it is nothing less than the energy of God, the Creator. And yet, at this time, as you are aware, there has been a great activation of this energy. You could say it is time for the Earth to graduate and it is preparing for a final examination. So if you feel at times almost overwhelmed by this energy, you are. But know always that within your heart of hearts you have asked for these transformations that you are receiving, and for this we are eternally grateful. The power of this love is unfathomable. The depths of this light, coming directly from Source, through the Hierarchy, through all of the universe, beaming all the way through to the third dimension of reality, is so profound and brilliant. And it is always available to you.

The human mind and consciousness are like a receiver. They are also like a transmitter. We are asking you who are lightworkers at this time to become actively aware of this transmission that is flowing through, to tune yourselves to receive it and to share it for the betterment of this planet and all living beings in all universes. How's that for a job? Why do you think we call you light *"workers"*? Because you have some work to do! It can be very playful work. It can be most enjoyable. It is our hope that it will be. But I am here to tell you that you will do it — for this light is rather ruthless! It doesn't seem to care if you are having a bad day. It doesn't seem to care if your landlord is getting his rent on time. It doesn't seem to care about time at all. It only cares about you as an ascending light being. It cares, as we care, about the divine healing and union that is taking place. So, for you, there is no escaping it.

What is your role? How can you enjoy this process? How can you make the most of your stay here on planet Earth? Some of you, I am sure, have been trying to avoid confronting the energies of this world that are somewhat distorted at this time. And at times it is only wisdom to do so. And yet, you are here to serve, to channel through this energy, this love. As I said, you are like receivers, like radios. And we are transmitting — on a very high frequency — our very own radio broadcasts for your enjoyment. It is for you to adjust the dial that is within your own heart and consciousness to a higher frequency. Perhaps you've only been listening to a rock and roll station, or the "golden oldies." We have something that is very old, in fact, very ancient. It is up to you, the listening audience, to attune yourselves to this.

You know, you are walking down the street in this world, and whether you are aware of it or not, your body is receiving radio waves. All of the radio waves that are being broadcast are passing through your physical form. Lots of static, isn't it? And there are also the collective thought patterns, the thought forms of an entire city and race, also penetrating and passing through your beings. At times it may feel overwhelming. And yet, if you will attune to the higher frequencies, by activating that receiver that is within you, you can be tapped into the very purest energy of all. You can see the light, and hear the inner music, the sounds of God. You can feel the vibration that is not vibrating, that is the subtlest frequency, the most blissful in existence. It is your choice. My work, and the work of all of the Masters who are truly giving themselves to this process of transformation, is to assist humanity in getting their hands on the dial and learning how to use it. For it is vital that you have access to Spirit — not as a thought, not as a philosophy, but in reality. It is vital that you practice each day attuning yourself to this, for these are the frequencies that ultimately will transform you in the ascension process. Once you have learned to tune into that higher frequency within you, it is simply a matter of enjoying, experiencing, and sharing.

It takes time and commitment on your part. Your time is very precious, is it not? In the physical, mortal body you only get so much of it. Where you are going it is not so limited. There is not a break, as there has been, between life and death. There is only life, always expanding and evolving. And yet, for you who are still existing in the physical, time is most precious. Along with time, your attention. What are you looking at? What are you focusing on in your life? What are you giving your attention and your consciousness to? It is very important for you to be aware of this "time and attention" factor in your lives. Maybe in another lifetime you had the opportunity to be initiated on the path of spiritual growth and enlightenment. All of you have experienced this in other lifetimes or you would not be here, you would not be ready for this message with open hearts and minds. But in those times, perhaps, you did not feel the immediacy. Now you feel the immediacy. Now you feel the grace that flows through you when you begin to give yourselves to Spirit, when you take one or two steps in that direction. I am not speaking conceptually. When you are giving yourself to Spirit, your spirit will acknowledge this in ways that you cannot deny.

You could say our transmitters are now in the process of being turned up to full power. But there are still many beings walking around feeling as if everything is business as usual. They are on a different station. They are experiencing another frequency, another energy level, and they are learning from this what they need to learn. Be grateful you are ready to receive the higher teachings. Be grateful that it is no longer necessary for you to wander around in this world like robots, simply fulfilling the thought patterns that were laid down before you or taught to you by authority figures. Be grateful that you have an open heart and a consciousness that is ready to receive the next level.

Let's say there are two persons standing in a room. This is a hypothetical example. One person is experiencing the normal sensations of being in a physical form. They are thinking of something or other that they meant to do, or perhaps what they will do later. They are worrying about something or other. Perhaps they are observing the way they look in the mirror, checking themselves out, trying to hold their world together. The other person is standing right beside that one, but in a state of extreme bliss. What's the difference? One is having an experience that is so far beyond that they cannot even put it into words. They feel their being melting in union with the divine. The other does not even notice, or maybe notices that he is acting a little strangely. "He looks like he's on drugs. I think there's something wrong with this person." There is nothing wrong with being a God-intoxicated soul! There have been enough of them walking the face of this planet to teach you how it is done. Now it's your turn.

And you thought you were only coming to hear a talk. You didn't know it was a party! Well, the drinks are flowing within you — through the tops of your heads and through your heart centers— as my colleagues do their work of love and healing.

So what can you do, my dear ones? How can you assist? I'm taking it for granted that you do desire this transformation, that it does sound appealing to you to go beyond wherever you have been before. There is no limit, you see. Enlightenment is not a static condition. It is an ever growing, ever progressing state. You progress from one state to the next. You progress through dimensions, through different forms of manifestation on your upward spiral to the Source, on your way back home. So to facilitate this, the return that you have longed for, I recommend you give yourself each day to Spirit. Take some time to enter the inner world, the world of light. Your God-self is there. It is not to be found in external teachings. It is not to be found in these words I am speaking to you. These words are just fingers pointing back to you, into your heart, into the consciousness of light that has existed within you. It is for you to enter that light. Give your Higher Self that precious time, that precious attention, and see what happens. Take time to meditate. Just sitting in meditation, in stillness, and calling forth your divine Self and the Masters and guides that work with you on a regular basis will transform you.

There is no time limit. It need not take twenty years. For some it takes twenty minutes. Most of you are somewhere in between there. The challenge in doing this is great, for there is resistance, as you know. There is resistance in this planetary consciousness, in the thoughtforms of the world, and that resistance also exists within your egos. There is part of you that wants to maintain absolute control. And there is another part of you that knows the business of surrender.

There are many ways that are taught — many paths — and most are valid. You need to find what works for you. I will say only that all of these paths converge in the light. And that light is within you, and you can experience it directly by focusing your attention at the third eye (the sixth chakra) in meditation. You can experience the vibration that sustains all of creation, for it is sustaining you. It is directly connected to your own breath. In meditation, you can focus your attention on the sound of your own breath. If you will call for assistance, I will help you. All of the ways that human beings have attempted to experience God ultimately converge within the human body: in that light, in that vibration, in that heavenly sound. You see, in order to serve this world and fulfill your missions here, it is necessary for you to maintain this contact with Spirit in a very real way. It is necessary for you to break through the thoughtforms of limitation that are holding an entire planet in slavery. We are calling on you as Masters-in-disguise, Masters temporarily in physical, third-dimensional bodies, Masters who have the ability to interact with humanity in ways that we cannot. It is necessary for you to make that transformation, to blaze the trail.

The way I see it, it is going to require many miracles, and as time is running out, you are going to witness a lot of miracles in a very short time. For this transformation must occur, and soon. The Earth's transformation is taking place. It will not wait for those who are falling behind. The Earth mother has waited and sustained humanity for countless ages, and now it is her time to awaken. So these energies that are flowing through are activating the planetary awakening, the planetary ascension, and your personal growth and ascension also. You have to just ride these waves, you know. My cosmic surfers! Learn how to do it and you won't fall off so much. When you fall off you get wet. No harm done! You just have to get back on. No two waves are alike. No two breaths are alike. You can meditate on God for an entire lifetime, and you will always feel that you are just beginning. You will always feel that you are just scratching the surface of what is available to you. And you are, for it is infinite. The door that opens within you does not open onto a one- or two-foot-wide beam. It opens onto another dimension. It opens onto the pathway that goes direct to Source.

So, for a human being ... well, to look at them, they don't look like much, do they? Two arms, two legs, walking around, scratching their heads ... all of the things you do. Who would have known that the human being would be the crown of creation, the interdimensional doorway that leads directly to God? But once you have learned this in practice and experience, your life is never the same. You still walk around and talk and do your activities and still scratch your head from time to time, for your worldly responsibilities must be taken care of, yet you are also aware of something divine, something beyond. And in the midst of your day, perhaps that door will open just a crack, and you will feel that energy flowing through. The depths of this love, the sensation of it flowing through a human body, creates the experience of bliss. It creates the experience of being completely satisfied and out of time, in union with the Creator, even while you are sitting there with your two arms and two legs. This is available to you. Union, God-realization is available to you. It is your immediate goal.

So how are we doing? We are creating quite a vortex here. When we gather together, we pull out all the stops. You see, we have got you all in one place and we are going to use you. We are going to allow the energy to focus through your bodies and through your beings to heal your city and your world. You will receive a healing as a consequence of being here and being open.

There are many beings who are sharing teachings of new age ideas and philosophies, and of course we honor all who do so. But know that each of you have the responsibility — for yourselves — of connecting with me, with your guidance, and no one can do it for you. Now it is time to awaken. All paths converge in the light. To be a lightworker, you need to know what that light is. You need to be able to experience it. How can you work with something if you've never seen it and don't know it? And once you see it and know it, you won't have to work anymore because it works through you.

Human beings have a tendency to complicate matters, to make the spiritual path complicated with many difficult techniques or methodologies. Of course, you can use whatever you wish, whatever works for you. But my recommendation is that, considering where you are going is a very childlike, simple, innocent place, you will have to drop many of the trappings of spiritual practice in order to get through that gate within you. And upon arrival you will be as a little child, totally dependent on Spirit for everything. To the average person you will perhaps look like a very organized and functional human being, with your responsibilities and your work in this world. But in your heart you will know you are just a divine child, and things will become very simple for you. The answers that you need will be provided if you give yourself. Give yourself to the stillness, so we can get a word in edgewise! When your mind is going a thousand miles an hour, your guidance is still with you, but you will not be able to hear it or feel it. When your mind is at peace, there is that stillness, there is that beautiful presence, there are the answers you have sought.

So how do you like my motivational speech? I am reaching out to clientele all over the planet, through this channel and others, and through the "channels" present within each of your hearts. I would like to say that I am always available to each of you. Always, if you ask, I am overshadowing you. If you do not feel my presence in your life, you need only to go into that stillness where I exist in your hearts. For I long to relate to you. I can be in communion with you much more directly, as many of you know, than I can in a channeling session. And this is my longing, for we are family. You are my brothers and sisters, my fellow lightworkers, as well as my children. I have seen all that you have created in your Earth lives, all that you have accomplished, and I long now to assist you in your return home. Offer up all that you are and all that you have done, all that you will do, in each moment, and we will walk together through this world. And no matter how long it takes in time before your completion in the ascension experience takes place, you will have a sense of my presence, and a knowingness, and a joy. This I give you. You see, I have too much of it. I need to give it away. I am here to serve you.

I believe I have said most of what I wished to say, but if you have questions for me, I will open the floor. If it is highest wisdom, I will do my best to answer and to assist you. So please feel free to ask whatever you wish. I am here to serve.

*"I've known about ascension for about two months now.
It took me that long to integrate the ideas into my life.
But in other areas — say, career and relationships — I
feel detached, like anything not related to ascension is
just temporary and not as important. Or maybe I haven't
integrated well enough."*

Everything you have experienced is, for the most part,
what you were meant to experience and what you needed
to experience to learn. If you did not know the feeling of
separation, when the sensation of union begins you would
not be able to have a frame of reference to understand and
appreciate that. So your detachment from human life is
natural. Again, as you have said, it takes some time to
integrate. It is always a process of integration. You are
integrating each day, as the energies are stepped up and as
you are growing. So it is not unnatural for you to experience this detachment. It is not that you are not loving.
When you are detached, you are able to love divinely, with
less attachment and less control. You are also able to free
yourself from the expectations and entrapments of
thoughtforms.

You know, when you stand up and do something
different in this world, there are many who will criticize
you, question you, and tell you to get back with the program. Many of you have experienced this. Perhaps you
tried to tell someone you knew about ascension, and they
thought you were crazy. And you said, "I know I'm crazy,
but this is still true!" There's nothing wrong with being a
little crazy. Most of the great accomplishments of humanity have been done by people who were somewhat eccentric.
Those who go along with the patterns and thoughtforms
of the herd mentality will experience just that: the mundane. So integration will continue, but it will be more subtle
and more easily experienced. You will never go back to
your old ways of being. It is not unloving to have the
Creator's love as your number one priority. This is only
aligning with the way it was meant to be all along. If others

do not choose to have this alignment, to have this experience, then that is their choice. They have more learning to go through. But don't let anyone dissuade you from your focus. You don't need to share your thoughts and philosophies with all of the people you know, but you do need to share your *love*, which is *our* love. This can be done silently, even in the midst of your day-to-day life. In walking through your world, you can call forth the presence of the Masters and ask for a blessing for all human beings that you interact with. All beings are becoming Buddhas. Perhaps you could look at them that way. Even the dogs and cats. Even the birds in the trees. They are all becoming Buddhas, all on the evolutionary spiral of consciousness. So be a Buddha yourself and bless them all silently in whatever way they will receive it. Perhaps they are waiting for you to go ahead and blaze the trail. And if you hold back and continue to have a mundane sense of reality and don't give yourself to Spirit, then you are not helping them to grow either. You are only fortifying that belief in limitation. You see, you just have to ask a question and it gets me going again!

"Sananda, I want to thank you for coming into my life. But how do I explain this to my children?"

There is no need for you to confuse the issue with your limited explanations of it. It is an experience of love and light that they are fully prepared for. I think it is necessary only that you work with them as any mother would, with love and healing energies, with no sense of trying to control their understanding in any way. I think that those of you who have children are receiving teachings from *them*, rather than the other way around. You will become as little children in your consciousness, so take note! They don't worry so much, do they? Just love them. And know that in your love, I am there.

And I am feeling your presence also. We are reuniting the family. Take a look around you at all of these strange beings that are your brothers and sisters, beings that you have perhaps known before in other lifetimes. And you can have a hearty laugh at the disguises they are wearing this time: "Why on Earth did you choose to look like that? Oh, it looks like you needed some humbling!" You know, the sense of humor is your number one weapon in the battle against darkness. When you are having difficulty, when you are getting so serious about meditation that you can't do it anymore, that's when it's good to have a hearty laugh! You see, there are many strategies that you use to attempt to re-create divine union. But once you have experienced it, you realize you were always in divine union. You will look back at everything you have tried, all of the practices, and realize you were there all along. It's so subtle. So just have that perspective. Don't be attached to controlling your experience: "I must see more light." The light comes to you when you are ready for it. Believe me, we are having trouble holding it back. If we let it forth into each one of you all at once, you would become a bunch of babbling idiots! Not a very good advertisement for our work!

So again, we come back to the integration of these energies. There is no end to them, you see. The power of the Creator and the power you possess within you is truly awesome. But until you are aligned with Spirit, purified sufficiently to handle it, it will not come through. You must have patience with your process, and trust that it is unfolding. Ask only that you receive the maximum that you can integrate in each moment. And give yourself. If you can surrender totally, you can have a total experience, to whatever degree you are able to let go. It's sort of like floating downstream, actually. So don't make it such a work experience. When you sit to meditate, just say, "Oh good, now I don't have to do anything." In Japan and China, the Zen masters have a practice called "sitting quietly doing nothing." That's meditation: doing nothing so you can feel who you are in essence, prior to thought and action. When your mind is not busy creating, you are one with the source of all creation.

"What part does the ego play in either enhancing or detracting from this transformational process?"

The ego is necessary in order for you to function in the third dimension. The ego acts as a filter for Spirit. If Spirit was unfiltered and flowing through you, you would become dysfunctional. You would not be able to find the brake pedal when you needed it. So you do need to have that ego framework. And yet, over-identification with the ego as yourself is detrimental. You see where it has gotten humanity. Look at the world around you! It is a manifestation of ego-identification, of separateness. So, ideally, those on the spiritual path will choose to simply offer their egos up to the divine for purification. Those thoughtforms and limiting beliefs that you have held within you can be transmuted, and you will still be able to drive your car and do your work. There is a great deal of power that longs to come through the lightworkers. But it is not a power that can come through at the level of ego. There are many powerful egos in this world, and many of them are longing to be able to channel through spiritual power and grace because they feel they should be able to do this: "I am a powerful being. I am a highly evolved being. Why am I not channeling the Ascended Masters?" Well, perhaps they are not humble enough. Maybe the ego has not yet been purified. Or maybe they have the feeling of needing to always be in control. The experience of running energy through you from Source, whether it be in a channeling or healing or any other way, is totally a feeling of "free falling," of being out of control. And as ego always wants to be in control, it is not able to fully enjoy or partake of that experience. It can only experience the by-products: "Oh that was a good channeling. I can feel the love and peace inside of me." Ego can only comment on the experience. So, ultimately, the ego is to be loved just as you would love any aspect of yourself. It is to be accepted with unconditional love. Do not try to control or perfect or criticize it. The energies of Spirit will align a human being so that ego takes its rightful place. The ego is the navigator, but Spirit is the captain of the ship.

"When I do my healing work, balls of light strike my heart chakra. I was wondering how I can control this, because it's so startling. But it feels so incredible!"

Why would you desire to control it?

"Well, it's real jolting. It creates the most incredible state of bliss. But it is startling."

I'll tell you what you do. Simply call on Spirit and ask me and your other guides to bring through the energy of healing in such a way that it is more gentle and graceful for your physical, emotional, and mental bodies to accommodate. You will be able to run this energy through you more gently. And yet, if it continues to come through strongly at times, then just surrender to this. If you are in a state of surrender, there is very little you should do to control it. But ask before you do your healing work that the energies come through in a way that do not harm you.

"As I continue in my path of spiritual enlightenment, I'm approached by others who seek answers, and I have this desire to share this with them. I'm not sure how to do this without my mind getting involved. Is there some way to do this?"

I will give you some words of wisdom. These, of course, will be different than all of the other words we have been sharing with you this evening! In the Bhagavad-Gita it is written that a man should not give up the work that God gives him, even though it may not always be perfect — just as in every fire there is always some smoke. It is for you to know, as a prior condition to your giving answers, that nothing of any eternal value can be spoken in language. Nevertheless, that is one of the tools you have to work with, here. So from a state of humbleness say, "To the degree I have experienced it, thus far on my path, this is what it feels like to me." Make sure that others always know it is your experience you are sharing. And then, you see, you can feel free to let Spirit come through you without having to control it or criticize it as it comes through.

There is no such thing as a perfectly clear communication when a being is in a physical form. There is simply too much static, too many thoughtforms. In our channeling, we have often said there is no such thing as a perfectly clear channeling. It is for each of you to take into your hearts the energies and words that are coming through, and see what is true and valuable for you. So you can do the same in your life. Call upon me to assist you in connecting with your heart energy. If you are coming from love and compassion, your words will find their truth in the heart. So just work on your beingness; neither seek for nor avoid interactions with human beings that want to hear what you have to say. Just offer your life to God and let him use you however he will. And he will. You will feel the union taking place and you will find it much easier as it goes along. Your integrity is to be honored here. So honor yourself. Many would like to have your experience. Maintain humbleness.

You know, the farther you go along the path, the easier it becomes to be humble. The farther you go, the farther you *have* to go, it seems. The more your awareness expands, the more you are aware that you are just beginning. So, innocence and purity are so important for lightworkers. Get the ego out of the way. Surrender it. You are not here to prove anything or convince anyone of anything. You are simply here to experience this transformation, so that others can witness it and experience it also. That is your primary service: just experiencing the transformation. That is your mission of the moment. It doesn't get much simpler than that.

"Are we getting close to having the necessary numbers for the ascension?"

There has been a great awakening in the past several years. There has been a vast shift in the energy, especially among the lightworkers. I recommend that you not think of it in terms of gathering together enough lightworkers, but rather of reaching the perfect critical mass. This is not dependent on numbers but on energy. This completion will occur in God's time, at the perfect moment for each human being.

"Sananda, can you comment upon the Earth changes that seem to be increasing in magnitude and frequency at this time?"

What is occurring on a planetary scale is a great clearing, a great balancing of discordant energies that have collected here upon this planet for many, many centuries. It is a time that requires a complete balancing of all karmic accounts. You could say the Earth has been giving you credit for quite a while, and now she is commanding that the debt is paid. The Earth has been holding negative energies, dense energies of human creation, and now is releasing these. In all cases, the beings who are affected by these releases are those who have been involved in creating these negative energies. So let this put your mind at ease a bit, when I say that there are no accidents, that you who are of the light have nothing to fear. The karmic balance is being carried out most efficiently and effectively by the Spiritual Hierarchy, and by the nature spirits. It is a beautiful concert, which to third- and fourth-dimensional thinking might seem a bit discordant, but is in truth in total harmony with what is required now.

There are natural laws in effect. You witness these each day in your lives, the laws of action and reaction. In order that balance can be achieved and the Earth can go into its next phase, into its fifth-dimensional manifestation, this karma is being cleared. This is what you are witnessing in the "Earth changes" phenomenon. And this is what you are experiencing also within yourselves, as your own beings come into balance and harmony.

Within this panorama, there is an additional power, an additional force that you may have not calculated into the equation. It is the power of grace. The power of grace can transform and transmute your karmic balance sheet. Each of you have, through your own creations, through your own beliefs, accrued certain karmic balances. For most of you I would say this balance is a very positive one. Yet still, all must be cleared in preparation for the liberation that comes with the final union with the Christ Consciousness.

Natural law, karmic law, has provided that human beings have had a certain time period in which to explore the realm of karma, of birth and rebirth, and death and re-death, in the search for the deeper reality, for that which is beyond. Now it is time for these experiments in consciousness to come to fruition. Whatever you have gathered in all of your lifetimes, there you have it! You have no more need to gather lifetime after lifetime of data as to what it is like to live in third-dimensional limitation. You have experienced this fully, have you not?

So you have a choice, dear ones, as to your alignment. In the spiritual path there is liberation, the transmutation of karmic patterns; there is freedom. Rather than having to live through these patterns and act out these balances and imbalances, now you have the opportunity to transcend this. This is a great blessing, and we are counting on you to open and receive it.

"Lord Sananda, I have heard from another channel that some people on planet Earth have already ascended and are preparing the way for the rest of the lightworkers. I'd like you to comment on that, please?

Yes, beings have ascended, of course, and we are preparing the way for you. You could say that those who have gone before have trod a very steep path to achieve the ascension, and in doing so have blazed the trail to make it easier for the remnant of the lightworkers to follow.

"I'd like to clarify my question. The information that I heard was that this has happened very recently. So I'm not necessarily referring to Masters such as yourself, but those who perhaps — during our lifetime — walk on the planet."

A very few, and never the ones who are making claims.

"Lord Sananda, when people start ascending, will there be large numbers, or will there be a few here and there?"

That remains to be seen, doesn't it? How would you like to create it? Probably as soon as possible, yes? I would say from my perspective, in all probability, there will be a few and then there will be a great wave, several great waves. I don't wish to limit it. I don't wish to put it out as a prediction. For that will create within you a belief system, and then you will feel the need to follow this belief system. So I would suggest that you view the path as a process you engage in every day of your life, but also one that will be completed by a great wave of grace, which will trigger a mass ascension, several waves of mass ascension. At those times it will be much easier and many will hopefully make the trip.

"What will happen if we ascend? Will we disappear?"

It will appear this way to the naked eye, to the casual observer. For those experiencing ascension, it will appear that the world around you is disappearing, with a new world appearing as you enter the higher dimension.

"Is there anything that we can take into the physical body to enhance and assist in meditation?"

I would say all sensible dietary patterns will assist you in your process. You cannot eat your way into ascension, but you can eat your way into a more difficult transition into the ascended state. Try not to take into your bodies dense energies in the form of alcohol, drugs, cigarettes, caffeine, etc. Whatever you can do to purify your diet and to eat more of the natural, life-giving foods is beneficial. You do not have to become a full-fledged vegetarian, but some move in that direction would also be helpful. Whatever your spirit guides you to, accept that as your next step. If your spirit guides you to a certain type of therapy for emotional release, dive into that and know it is part of your ascension path. If you are guided to become one who fasts one day a week, or one day a month, or drinks more vegetable juices, try that. Each of you are individuals and your own spirits will guide you in the directions you need to go. That is why I recommend you sensitize yourself to Spirit and let that guide you. I will not write out a prescription for each of you individually; it would not be practical. You see how much more practical it is for each of you to connect with your guidance. So trust your body's judgment. Just feel it. Sit down and feel your body and ask it what it wants to eat. Maybe you will be surprised. Maybe you will receive a channeled message from your own body telling you not to do this anymore, or that it would prefer more of this. Truly, it is much easier to meditate if you don't drink eight cups of coffee first! I will go so far as to give you that prescription. More and more your bodies will be taking their nourishment from Spirit. More and more, you will be feeding from light and love.

So, perhaps we could spend a few minutes doing some energy work. We are aware that you have a certain attention span. If we use up your attention span before we get to the meditation, it is not as effective.

Throughout this day, we have been sharing with you energetically. The energies are being transmitted from higher dimensions, focused through many Masters, through the light vehicle overhead, and through your heart centers. In closing this days' activities, we ask that you offer yourselves in a few moments of silence, so that we can intensify the energy a bit in ways that will greatly enhance your ability to interact with Spirit and receive the healing that you require. Whatever your next challenge is, you can also offer that up and we will work with you directly. So just relax and breathe. Focus on your breath or on the inner light, whatever is easiest for you. We will enhance the energy field around you that will open your heart chakras and balance you. We will do this in silence. I ask that you just relax and allow for a few moments.

I would like to close this meditation with a few affirmations. I would like to ask you to repeat several times, in silence, the following affirmations:

I AM light.

I AM love.

I AM peace, in harmony with all.

I AM the open door.

I and the Father are one.

I AM that I AM.

So, my dear friends, it is time for me to say farewell for this day. You may, of course, be with me in meditation for as long as you wish. Again, I thank you for sharing your precious commodities of time and attention. I offer you each individually, with no exceptions, my full support and love on your path. And you may trust in that and give yourself to that. If you have challenges, or times when it is difficult to focus and feel Spirit, call upon me and I will do all that is within my power for you in each moment. The time of separation is over. It is time for that connection, for communion. We are counting on each of you, in the openness of your hearts and the longing and devotion you have within yourselves to fulfill your Earth missions, to make that transformation and to offer yourselves in that way. And enjoy it. It is not always enjoyable, but it is meant to be enjoyed. And as those challenges are surpassed, you will recognize that even those are gifts and blessings. I thank you for allowing my energies into your beings. It has been a very blissful experience for me, as well. Good day.

CHAPTER TWO

THE DIVINE BLUEPRINT

❧ St. Germain ❧

Good evening, dear friends. This is St. Germain. I come to you this evening with love and light, to shower you with grace and blessings, to bring through my presence and the presence of all the Masters who are in attendance. We come to nurture and support you on your spiritual path, in your lives here on this planet Earth. The work that we will do this evening will be — for the most part — energetic, though I will also share with you in language, to keep your minds occupied while we are working with you. You could look at this evening as one long guided meditation.

Truly, words cannot express — never have been able to express, never will *be* — the truth, the reality that exists within each of you, within each atom of creation. The power and majesty of the light of Source, of the Creator, exists in every atom of this creation. You as human beings, as human tuning forks, are beginning to resonate with this frequency, this powerful message of love that is flowing through — direct from Source, channeled through the many beings of the Spiritual Hierarchy, all the way into third-dimensional Earth experience. You could say the universe is re-tuning one of the instruments of the orchestra that has been in disharmony.

So relax and enjoy yourselves this evening, my friends. I am overjoyed to be with you, with so many gathered together, feeling the intensification of this time that you are sharing, this time that you have chosen to manifest in physical form here on planet Earth (though at times you may wonder why indeed you chose to!). That will all be made clear, if it is not so already. We are going to clear away the cobwebs, so that you can recognize who you are and why you are here. Indeed, you are multidimensional beings, not at all limited to this physical form. But we have noticed a tendency for you to get a little bit caught up in that. At this one level of your beings, there seem to be a few knots yet to work out.

Your divine overself, your God-presence, the I AM Presence overshadowing each of you, is a perfect model of divinity. You could say that there is a divine blueprint for this creation. We call it the divine plan. And there is a divine blueprint within each being. Where there has been misqualified energy with regards to either the divine plan or the individual blueprint within each of you, there is the need for realignment.

Indeed, I do not think that the Creator would recognize this world based on the divine plan that he intended for it. You see, there were "architects" that looked at this divine plan and thought, "Well, that looks quite good, but I think it can be improved upon." So they set about with their erasers and their pencils, making a few subtle changes. And that's what we are here trying to clean up. There is always someone who thinks they know better, that they can do it better. Someone who can't leave well enough alone. Someone who longs to take something that is perfect and color it, or make it their own, rather than simply observing and enjoying and allowing the flow.

So, planet Earth, as you are well aware, has been affected by some of these dysfunctional patterns. And as you are also aware, the cycle wherein these dysfunctional patterns have been allowed to manifest is coming to a close. Now the cosmic conductor is realigning and re-tuning this divine instrument, this planet Earth, this solar system, this universe, and this physical being that you call your self.

The tools that are being used for this divine operation are very simple. They are love and light and the many manifestations of these. Empowered by grace, many beings on this world are now attuning to the master pitch, the master tuning fork. Many are in agreement that it is time to come into realignment, to bring this world back into harmony with Spirit. And indeed, you are here also as manifestations of that very same love and light and grace. You are the lightworkers who are here to alter those negative patterns, to replace them with that which is positive and healing, to break through and erase those old dysfunctional patterns.

In order that the healing of this world may take place, it is necessary for the operation to be accomplished at every dimensional manifestation, including here in the physical world. That is why you have, in your wisdom, chosen to manifest as physical beings. If this operation could be accomplished from higher dimensions, it would be done so. But it was necessary for beings of light and power to descend into matter, to raise the physical into alignment as well. At every dimension there are beings ministering to this planet. Many of us you are aware of, many more of us you are not. There is so much grace flowing, you could say the world is being overwhelmed with it. Sometimes, on your path, you feel dysfunctional yourself. Sometimes there are negative emotions to be cleared. Sometimes it feels overwhelming even to be here, just to be alive on this world, let alone to accomplish anything. Just making it from one day to the next can be quite a challenge. This is why we have recognized your need for inspiration, healing energies, and guidance. This is why there is such a thing as channeling, and such a thing as avatars incarnating in physical bodies, and many other divine manifestations. For though you are very powerful, though the divine blueprint of your mighty I AM Presence is magnificent to behold, still there is a tendency to identify only with the limited physical, mental, and emotional side.

You could say it is similar to one of those experiments in a laboratory, where they place the white mouse in a maze. The white mouse can't get up and look down upon the maze; he can only stumble from one hallway, one corridor to the next, to find his way to the cheese. In your case, substitute "ascension" for cheese! So we are here to inspire you with a higher perspective, so that you can raise your consciousness to a point where you are looking down at the maze, so you can easily see how to get to that cosmic cheese!

So, as we have said, with all the grace and love and light available to you, and with the tools at your disposal to focus on these energies in your spiritual practice, you will be raised to a higher perspective, a higher consciousness. On your path to the ascension experience, you will pass through many doorways, have many experiences. Many of these experiences have been labeled by spiritual orders in the past. Some of these experiences are quite uniquely your own. You are in the process of aligning with the divine blueprint that is present within you, and the physical body is also being aligned with that. Oftentimes it feels a little uncomfortable, does it not? You feel your atoms and molecules wiggling around. The divine blueprint exists within each of you, and it is the blueprint to your own ascension. It is a blueprint that existed before you manifested as a physical human being. It is a blueprint that is far older within you. And in every human life, through all of the experiences you have chosen in all of your lifetimes, there have been subtle modifications to this blueprint.

Ultimately, you each have a unique pattern to follow, to become. That is why we do not tamper with your individual paths. We can give you guidance concerning meditations, and practices that will help you raise your consciousness. But your path to the ascension, through God-realization, is unique. You are each unique jewels in the crown of the Creator.

So, you could say, my dear friends, that it is coming down to the wire here. Those of you who have been on your path for some time are probably aware of the intensification that is occurring. It is an intensification of grace, of love and light. It also may manifest within you as an intensification of your process. You see, what is causing you these processes is an increase of love and light. Sometimes you feel that the love and light desert you, when in fact you are being flooded with it. You are learning to align with and accept it. It is raising you to a higher level of awareness.

I ask that you view all of your situations, all of your apparent problems and concerns, from a higher perspective. Know that your divine blueprint creates and causes you to experience everything you have and will experience. And you take these experiences with you in purified form, in the form of wisdom, back with you into the higher dimensions as you return.

We have said many times in our gatherings that the time of increased intensification of the manifestation process is at hand, and certainly it is here. I think you will notice within your own individual lives, and within the overall life of this world, a great quickening of the process. That which is of karma within you is being released, via manifestation or purification, just as the karma of this world and all beings upon it is being played out. It is all a part of the divine drama. We are asking you each to assume full responsibility for the manifestations you experience in your lives, for your own existence here, and indeed for your role as lightworkers. It is increasingly important that each of you access your own spirit, and through this, the Source of all. It is more and more important that you take your spiritual path beyond intellectual and philosophical pondering into the direct experience of God and all of his manifestations. I will say all of "her" manifestations, for the goddess worshipers! You have to watch out with this language. You'll get a bad reputation! "Don't you think Saint Germain was rather chauvinistic this evening? I would have thought he would have been beyond all of that."

So how can you as individuals take advantage of this opportunity? The opportunity to experience a rebirth into the higher dimensions, via the ascension, is available to you. In fact, now is your chance, you could say. The doors are open. You apply for this experience in your heart, and you offer that heart up to the Creator with humility and acceptance and trust. Also, we will have a sign up sheet afterwards, in case you don't really believe there is anyone there listening to your prayers! Some of you want to see it in writing. You know you have a contract that has already been signed. It has been notarized by Sananda himself. We are calling on you to fulfill your contract as lightworkers. I do not think you want to face litigation! You don't want to be brought up before the karmic board: "Well, Mr. Klein, you were scheduled for God-realization in 1993, and here it is 1994. You are deviating from your divine blueprint. What have you got to say for yourself?" "Well, I was doing the best I could." That's the oldest excuse in the book. After all of these lifetimes, can't you think of something more creative? The second most common one is "The dark forces hindered me. I was well on my way, but I met with interference." Your excuses also will be consumed in the divine flame. All that is not of joy and love and light will be consumed.

When all of those old patterns are consumed, there will be nothing left but you, your Higher Self. And in the moment that you have that perspective, there will be only the awareness of divinity, of union. That is a good platform from which to operate. If you are caught up in patterns of duality: "Oh, this is good, and this is bad. This is darkness, and this is light," and always trying to walk the tightrope, staying in the Light, judging that which is other — soon you will come to realize that what you have been judging is also your teacher, your guru, and also a manifestation of the Oneness that Is. Enlightenment is simply a consciousness that is beyond duality, where pleasure and pain are one, where you experience oneness, union, within all of these patterns of existence and manifestation. The physical form is still walking around in a physical world, bumping up against all of the strange challenges you have to face. And yet, within, there is an awareness of the Oneness — an absolute knowingness of the divinity of every experience, a surrender to every experience as a manifestation of the divine blueprint. I think you are all in for some wonderful surprises.

So, let's get practical for a moment here. What can you as an individual do at this time, in this moment, in this lifetime, to achieve the completion of your path to enlightenment and ultimately to ascension? It is extremely important, as we have said, for each of you to learn to access Spirit, to access the divine aspect of yourself. I recommend that — with humility, with honesty — you go within in your lives and ask, "Is there anything more I can do as an individual, as a lightworker, to accelerate this path of growth, and to serve as I am intended to serve." For without that experience of Spirit, without a sense of purpose, you will feel lost. You will witness the purification of karma on this world, in your being, and in people around you. If you have no sense of purpose, if you have no anchor in the light, you will feel lost and confused. If you have learned, or are open to learn, how to meditate and focus on Spirit and give yourself to that, how to surrender in your life to whatever is highest wisdom, you will reap the rewards and blessings — indeed, blessings that are far beyond what you can even dream of.

For while we cannot truly express in language what we are experiencing, or what you are about to experience, we can definitely say that it is "beyond." It is so filled with love, light, and joy to finally be free, and it is your fortunate state to be ones who are on that path to freedom. In fact, it is your service. It is the purpose, the main purpose that you incarnated in physical form: to show others how to attain that liberation. If you do not attain it, you are not fulfilling your mission, your purpose in being here.

So, we ask — indeed *recommend* — an increase in your individual commitment to Spirit. Wherever you are now is where you must begin. If you are not practicing meditation, perhaps you could begin. If you are, perhaps you could experiment. Try giving yourself in a more focused way for a longer time. Throw yourself up into the light. If you throw yourself up there enough times, pretty soon you're going to stick! Truly, that's when the fun begins. Not that this isn't enjoyable, what you are all experiencing here, but there is so much more. So give yourselves, dear ones, to the fulfillment of your individual divine blueprint, your own spiritual path to the ascension. Know that your path is unique. You don't have to do it the same way that someone else is doing it, though you do have to have an open mind, an open heart, to learn from what others are experiencing. Don't be afraid to experiment in your lives.

If you are unfamiliar with the Ascended Masters, with working with us in meditation, try an experiment. Try something new. Before you meditate, say "Saint Germain, please be with me. Please help me in this meditation." I will assist you, along with any of the other Masters that are appropriate.

You are never alone on this path. There is a story from India, of a devotee standing in heaven alongside his guru. They are looking down on the Earth, at all the paths the devotee walked in his lifetime. And the devotee looks at the path and says "I see in these places where we were walking together, where there are two pairs of footprints, and it was beautiful. And then I see places where there is only one set of footsteps, and those were the times when I was going through difficulty and felt lost and alone. Where were you, my teacher, when I needed you?" And the teacher turns to the devotee and says "That's when I was carrying you!" Truly, you are never alone.

There is a little bit more work I would like to do with you this evening. I would like to do some violet flame work to assist you in your processes. But before we do so, if any of you have questions in areas you would like me to address, we will take a few moments for this.

"I have a question. In another organization that I was in, we used to spend hours doing "Violet Flame" as a group, doing chants and decrees, and from the tapes that I've heard from this group, we're basically just saying that we are one with the violet flame and that's sort of doing it. Is it beneficial to spend concentrated amounts of time with the Violet Flame for personal and planetary healing? Or are they just two different functions, two different groups?"

It's all the same to me. If it feels better to do hours and hours, if you have the time, do so. I would say to experiment. You can tell when it clicks. So do it until you feel it click.

"My wife and I wanted to go to a restaurant for three years and never had time to do it ... finally we got a chance to go when she gave me The Crystal Stair *to read as a gift. I got really excited and wanted some kind of confirmation that this was really happening in my life. Then we finally went to this restaurant and I was looking out the window and saw the street sign, and the restaurant was on Ascension Street!"*

The moral of the story is that good things are worth waiting for!

"My husband has chosen a body that apparently has Alzheimer's now. Are there ways that I can assist him in following the path to the ascension?"

Number one, follow it yourself. Do not allow your grief or sorrow to interfere, or allow it as little as possible to interfere with your spiritual practice. In your spiritual practice, in your meditations, call upon myself and Lord Sananda, Mother Mary, the other Masters that you work with, and your love and light to surround his physical form. Just visualize it rising, visualize it glowing, and this will do a great deal to assist. You cannot control another's spiritual path, another's divine blueprint. So you must detach from your desire, if you have one, to do so. Ascension is an individual experience. Even though it may occur as a mass exodus, still each being will experience it as an individual spiritual experience.

"I have a question. There is still a lot of mind chatter in my meditations, so I'm really dissatisfied. What's going on?"

You are not alone. The channel has been having a lot of mind chatter, too. Indeed, he was feeling that he would not even be able to channel this evening, because he felt too crazy! He contemplated putting a sign on the door: "Dysfunctional patterns have prevented me from channeling this evening. My apologies." There will be times for all of you when the energies coming in will be rather challenging to cope with. There is a shifting going on within you. I would say simply to do the best that you can, and ask for assistance. Perhaps you could spend some time grounding in nature, that sort of thing. Take it outside of your usual pattern. You have a usual habit of meditation. Generally your mind is ready and waiting to ambush you there. But if you will surprise it — you could say, "out-flank" the mind — by sitting down and meditating in an unexpected moment, you can catch it by surprise before it has time to reload. It is all part of the path. Nothing to be overly concerned about. Your dissatisfaction must also be surrendered. It does not mean you are going backwards. It does not mean you are not doing it right. In fact, if you do it right you will encounter many such obstacles and challenges, and they will all be overcome. Sometimes you just have to sit and cry, and pray for help.

> *"In that period of time in sleep where it feels like you're awake, I've been having some experiences of being physically attacked at those times, where it doesn't feel like a dream but a direct experience. The only way I can get out of it is to call for help from Jesus, and then I get pulled right out of it. Sometimes in that state, I can't remember to do that, and the last couple of times have been quite assaulting and scary. Do you have anything to say about that?"*

First of all, assume responsibility for attracting these energies, though do not assume blame or guilt over it. Know that it is part of your divine blueprint to learn to deal with it. Then, upon assuming full responsibility for everything that you have created in your existence, call for Archangel Michael to surround you with his light and blessings. Ask that if there are any invisible beings around you, tending to hover around you in your life, ask that they be taken into the light, into their proper places, and ask them simply to go in peace. If you will do this, it will help a great deal. Many beings are attracted to you lightworkers, many fourth-dimensional beings. It is not necessarily a psychic attack. It is simply that these beings are watching you and trying to learn something. You see, they learn more from observing the physical realm, feeling that they are still somehow connected to it. So those of you who are rising in frequency and light may tend to attract these beings for healing, and they can even rise following your lifestream into a higher manifestation. You could view yourself as an energy vortex, swirling upwards, that these beings — like moths — are attracted to. And when they get into the flame, the vortex, they are swept upwards into the light.

"Has the first wave of ascension occurred yet?"

We wish! We are waiting, just as you are. Don't be attached to when, how, or any of the details. Just give yourself to Spirit, and watch. It will occur when it is perfect for you.

"I have a four-year-old son who, since age two, has voiced great fears of what he calls ETs, and many of us have thought that there might be beings around him. Could you speak about the children and how to deal with their sensitivities?"

If you are not afraid, chances are the child will not be afraid. Many times, a child takes its reflection of what is appropriate to believe from the reflections he or she receives. So if you were to act as if this was nothing to fear, as if it were just a part of life, this would help. Know that you are always surrounded by higher-dimensional beings. There are many who can see them, many who can feel them, many who can hear them. There will be many more, especially the children that are born now. These are ones who have their filters less developed, their blinders, you could say. You might find them having quite a conversation with someone that you can't even see. So it is part of the child's path, also. I would say to share love and reassurance, and just allow. And don't hold any negative feelings yourself, or fear about it. Call upon Archangel Michael and the other Masters to surround you and your child with their light and protection, and that will help to ward off any negative entities. If there are positive entities, they will not feel frightening, but joyful.

"I was alone in the house the other night, and I'm pretty sensitive and I heard a lady's voice say 'Heaven' in a very strong commanding voice. Was that an angel talking from a higher dimension?"

Yes. Most of the time human beings do not listen to their angelic guardians. They might hear a voice, but it is so fleeting and the mind and ego take over and cover it up. When you become more sensitive, you can receive many different signals, voices, and blessings. So that was a blessing for you. There will be many more blessings.

"In their divine plan, does each entity have a plan, an Earth time when they are going to awaken? Sometimes we want to share with our loved ones and they are not receptive to it. Is it just not their time yet?"

Well, that is rather a complex issue. If someone is not yet open to spiritual guidance in the way you are, you could indeed say it is not their time yet. But there is no specific point in time when a human being is scheduled to suddenly awaken and begin to feel Spirit. It is more a matter of grace and inspiration, though each being (in the completion of their karma) will come to a point where there is a bit more clarity, where there is a bit more balance, and this will in effect draw forth new, more subtle experiences. Though for practical purposes, it is not a bad way to look at it: that it is not their time yet.

"Do I need to do any work with my eight-year-old son regarding the ascension, meditations, or just let him be a little boy?"

Let him be a divine eight-year-old! He is here to teach *you*. He will teach you how to surrender, and many other valuable lessons which you can apply to your ascension path. Just love; just love. The children do not need programming; they just need love. You would all be better off if you had only received love, would you not? I might not even have had to make this stop tonight! So, do unto them as you would have hoped someone would have done unto you.

So, it is time for me to begin to think about leaving, so I would like to do a bit of energetic work with you this evening. I would like to share some work with the violet flame this evening — the all-powerful, transmuting energy of grace that can assist you in your path, in clearing old karmic patterns, dense energies, for you and for this planet. So just for a few moments, we will meditate together. Just sit and relax and breathe. Don't try to go anywhere, don't try to be anything. Just relax and breathe. Feel the breath moving in and out of your body in a relaxed and natural way. This is God talking to you. When you learn to understand that language, your troubles are over. Know that you are surrounded by many beings of blessed light, that this gathering is surrounded by love and light. Know you are safe and protected within this beautiful sanctuary, in which you can relax and be yourself, your divine Self.

I would like to ask you to visualize a beautiful column of violet light, slowly descending through the center of our circle — a beautiful radiant, powerful, pulsating column of light descending down through the floor and into the center of the Earth, a beautiful energy vortex. Into this column of light, I ask each of you to take a few moments to offer all negative energies, all obstructions and obstacles to your growth, all negative emotions, whatever it is that you have felt may be hindering you in your process. Just offer it into the center of the light. Let it be dissolved and carried upwards. And now I would like you to visualize this beautiful light column slowly expanding, becoming wider and wider, until it surrounds your bodies and this entire gathering with a beautiful, healing, violet energy. Allow this light energy to fill every cell of your body. Offer up all resistance. Let's just sit for a few moments in this energy ...

Now I ask you each to visualize the column slowly condensing once again towards the center of the circle. And as it rises, it carries with it all impurities and dense energies, leaving you feeling light, peaceful, and full of love for yourself and for all beings. And I ask that the effects of this work that we have accomplished this evening go forth to benefit all sentient beings of this planet, and that this work be permanently sealed and in effect for all time. So be it!

So, my dear friends, I thank you this evening. It has been very enjoyable for me to be with you. I thank so many of you for coming out into the winter night to be with me this evening. It is a very hopeful sign. Continue to give yourselves to Spirit. Love yourselves. Don't be self-judgmental or critical, but do be honest. Where you can improve, do so. And see what happens. The time is here now when you can manifest — and you will manifest — all the blessings and all the rewards of your spiritual work. Until we meet again, good night.

CHAPTER THREE

THE PURE OF HEART

⋘ Archangel Michael ⋙

Greetings, my dear ones. This is Archangel Michael. I have a great energy feeding to share with you this evening. A beautiful ray of love, light, healing, and higher perspective for each of you. I ask that you focus yourselves intently, relax your bodies, and be at ease. None of you are here by accident.

So how are you enjoying your process these days? Tonight we are here to process along with you in a very beautiful and peaceful way, yet with the full intention of elevating you, lifting your consciousness and the vibrational frequency of your beings to new heights. Later on you can tell me how successful I was.

I would like to discuss a little bit about this process you are undergoing, the experiences that you are having, with emphasis upon your work as lightworkers and teachers here. For it is time for those of you who are possessed with the abilities to be as teachers and lightworkers to move into another phase, as truly the planet moves into another phase of transformation. Each of you are lightworkers, to a certain degree. Each of you have capacities and talents.

Some of you have barely scratched the surface of that which you have to share of your spiritual gifts. Others are well on their way in manifesting these.

There is a process that you are all engaged in. It is a purification process, especially for those of you who are giving yourselves to service as teachers and healers in this world. There is an energy coming through, which will continue, which has been very activational for you, and has indeed been a test, a challenge, a purification of the motivations and perspectives of your own heartfelt desires. Your capacities for discernment, sensitivity, compassion, and surrender are being tested, challenged, and brought to the forefront of your consciousness. For now it is time, my dear ones, for you who have labored in the shadows of this world, for you who have given yourselves with sincerity to the spiritual path, to begin more and more to step forward as healing channels of the divine. It is in this beautiful moment that holds so much promise for each of you that I have chosen to speak on this subject.

There is a purification which takes place for one who is preparing and giving themselves to service. There is a self-examination that takes place as one is tested in sincerity and detachment, surrender, and trust. Many have and many will continue to have opportunities placed before them, opportunities brought to their consciousness and to their field of operation by the activity of the Higher Self, in conjunction with the many Masters that serve you. Many opportunities are coming your way. It is your free will as to whether you will accept or reject each of these. And yet, these opportunities are of a divine nature. They are opportunities to be lightworkers, teachers, and healers, not only in thought, but in deed. It is a time that you have awaited, a time that you have looked forward to. The veils around your consciousness will be removed to reveal who you are and what you are here to achieve. Truly it is a wondrous time. And we enjoy so much the experience of the awakening of the lightworkers, those who have slept within the apparent separation of the physical body.

There is a promise here that is unfolding. It is truly something which has not occurred before. There have been many Masters who have walked upon the face of the planet, but never have there been so many awakening simultaneously, having such a tremendous effect. And as we witness this and assist this process, we are amazed at the light that you bestow upon this world and upon those beings that you encounter. The process that engages many of you is one of purification, of self-examination, of subtle adjustments in your perspective. All of this aligns and focuses you so that when these powerful energies of Spirit come through you, you will be prepared to receive and channel them through in many ways, for many purposes. For the light that does wish to come through at this time is very, very profound. The light is very strong, and requires of one who works with it a true alignment, a purification of the spiritual bodies as well as within the physical body and the personality.

Where there is ego attachment there will be friction, there will be obstruction. Where there is surrender and innocence, there will be glorification and exultation. The light is coming through every lightworker at this time to the maximum degree that each is capable of bringing it through. And I do not mean only those who channel in this way, but all who channel from the deepest Self in whatever form. Where there is manipulation, where there is an over-predominance of spiritual pride or egotism, the light will diminish. Where there is innocence and purity and sincerity, the light will be magnified many, many times. So if you are one who has been undergoing difficulties or challenges, I share the perspective that perhaps there is a purification taking place which will ultimately allow more grace to flow through you. Perhaps you could say your Higher Self has been preparing you for that which is to come.

What is to come is beginning. It is growing and escalating in power. Only those who have the eyes to see, only those who have surrendered themselves fully to Spirit, will gain true perspective as to what it is that is occurring in this world. All will experience it, but each individual will have their own unique perspective. Those of you who have been practicing your surfing, riding these waves of grace, will gain expertise which will allow you to maintain balance no matter how large the waves may become. If you have been practicing riding on these waves, then that which I am speaking of now will be no great surprise to you. If you have not, you may find yourself feeling a bit overwhelmed at times. For the light of God does not hesitate, but washes over all equally. It does not discriminate, but loves all equally.

You are ones who will, through your experience, be as examples for others who may be feeling overwhelmed, demonstrating how to ride these waves of grace, how to integrate these energies. It is an opportunity for the lightworkers to step forward onto the world stage, to assume responsibility for their own experience, and to share that in whatever way they are guided. You have been prepared, all of you, for many lifetimes for just this time, or you would not be here with me this evening. There is no limit to what you can experience, my dear ones. Those who have realized the role of service will understand that the more you open and surrender to Spirit and allow yourself to be a servant of the Higher Self, and ultimately of the Creator, the more grace and bliss and enjoyment you will have. The more love and light you bring through, the more wide open you will become. The river of grace longs to flow through you. If you wish the maximum experience, you require the maximum purification, openness, surrender, and humility.

Great saints and yogis are very childlike and innocent. They are simply being who they are in each moment. And yet many beings come and sit at their feet to feel the presence of the Creator flowing through them. They don't think, from their perspective, that they are anything special, that they are doing anything special aside from being who they are. They have cultivated a purity, an openness, an ability to dive into the light. And in doing so, the light flows through them, just as it will flow through you more and more profoundly. As this begins to happen, it places a bit of a challenge upon your limited self-concepts. Each of you have a certain level of comfort around being world teachers. Some of you like to be behind the scenes. Some of you can't wait to get out on the stage. There are some who can't wait to get out on the stage, who will never have the chance because they are too involved on the ego level. There are others who have no desire, who have been behind the scenes, who will be pushed from behind and find themselves standing in front of an audience. Then what is your choice, but to be yourself? That is all that is ever required of you. You are never guided by Spirit to a position or situation that you are not prepared for.

In giving yourself to your practice of meditation, you will be lifted in your perspective. You will have a certain degree of objectivity with which to view the choices that you make, the experiences that you create for yourselves, and this is the process of self-examination. It is a very intense learning process that you are engaged in. One thing you are learning is that when you are not being inwardly directed by Spirit, you encounter more friction, obstruction, and difficulty. When you are surrendered to your inner Self, life flows much more easily, much more smoothly, and you are guided to the perfect situations to hear the perfect words that you have been perfectly prepared to hear. And you are ready for that. You open your heart to that. You are accepting life rather than controlling it.

Great changes are taking place. Have the eyes to see what is occurring now in this world and in these critical days. Know that the light will rise to the surface. Accept the challenge. If your motivation is pure, you will be guided along divine paths and you will have no need to fear. Each of you will have so many experiences, so many opportunities to share of yourselves. With all the lightworkers in this city, and all of the lightworkers on this planet, how many opportunities will each have to shower the light of the divine Self through into the third and fourth dimensions, so that beings who feel trapped in these dimensions can witness the opportunity that is available now, to go beyond, into liberation.

No being is ever truly imprisoned. The belief in imprisonment creates the experience of it. You are surrounded by beings who feel themselves imprisoned in the body form, in third- and fourth-dimensional thoughtforms. It is for you to be the ones to give another example. "Why not look in this direction, my friend? Here's something you may have overlooked." To break the pattern of limitation and imprisonment by simply not believing in it any longer is a wonderful service. The more beings who stop believing in imprisonment and limitation, the stronger the energy builds, the wider the doorway becomes for others to walk through. The space that you hold as lightworkers is no small thing. And though you may not give yourself to formal teaching, whatever it is you do in your life can be, in each moment, an acceleration for the planetary consciousness. If you but have the purity of heart and a perspective that is beyond limitation, then you are holding the door open for others to come through, just as we hold the door open for you.

Each human being is an interdimensional doorway. Within your hearts is a doorway that you open, and in that opening, light is showered into what was darkness. If you can keep your inner doorway open, and if many lightworkers will do the same simultaneously, that light will break the patterns, will reveal to the beings believing in limitation a new pattern of being, a new way of joy and freedom and peace that has been lacking on this planet. So take some time in your life, my friends, to go within and examine your motivation. Examine what is important to you and whether or not you are applying yourself to that. For it is time to go beyond the theories, to go beyond the mere thoughtforms of enlightenment into the actual practice and experience. In that practice, there is no room for fear or hesitation. There is never a moment when you cannot be acting as a divine servant to this world, for you have the breath meditation which holds the door of the heart open from moment to moment. And with each breath that you take, consciously, you allow Spirit to integrate more fully into this dimension. And with every opening of your heart, you allow for the opening of another.

It is a sympathetic reaction. If you take stringed instruments ... let us say you have two guitars. When you place them in front of one another, and strike a certain string on one guitar, the other guitar (which has not been struck) will also begin to vibrate and resonate at that pitch. And so it is with you: as you resonate the frequencies of light and love, the heartstrings of all of humanity are feeling this and are beginning to awaken. At first this occurs mainly on the subconscious level, and yet the Higher Self of each individual is taking note and amplifying this vibration of truth within. And you will witness many, many beings around you experiencing processes of opening and awakening that you have already passed through. And you will be ones who will reach back to console them. The patterns that you have broken of limitation, the patterns of abuse, the patterns of insensitivity and pain and sorrow that you have transcended, will act as a training for you in reaching back to assist others to do the same.

So it is a divine experience, a divine purification that is taking place. The work that you do upon yourselves, and the surrender that you allow in your hearts, is not for you alone: it affects all. It is critical now that you give yourselves to this purification process. Go within and surrender to the light. Meditate upon the breath, upon that light. It is important now. And don't be afraid to come up onto the stage if your number is called. When you have the opportunity to share your spirit, in whatever way, you will find that great quantities of light and energy will come through and sustain you and nourish you and support you in this strange new world you are entering, the strange new world of love, surrender, and liberation. You have all been there before, so it is not new to you. As you take up the mantle of your own divinity once again, it will come back to you. Your veils will be removed. You will recall at a cellular level, from the very essence of the Self, why you are here. You will begin more profoundly to have the effect that you desire to have.

So always, my dear ones, carry a prayer that you shall remain in light, that you shall remain surrendered to Spirit, that you shall remain pure of heart. For this is your divine ticket. This is what you can do. So many opportunities will be coming your way. Some of you already know of what I am speaking of. I encourage you in this little pep talk — before you go back out onto the world — to have faith in yourselves. Have faith that you are of the light, that you are a lightworker, that your motivation is pure. And let this be your foundation. And then when those clouds of ego come over your consciousness, clouds of attachment, control issues, or whatever, you will easily be able to release those and open to a new and more powerful manifestation, a more pure manifestation.

The choice is up to you, my dear ones. The gates of grace are open. The opportunity to serve is here before you. It is your free will as to what you will accept. Every great mission upon this Earth began in a very simple way, with a very simple step, with one tiny baby step after another. No saint has ever set out to become a great world teacher. Perhaps they set out to be happy. Perhaps they set out to be liberated from illusion, and found that on this path others began to look up to them and to pay attention to their actions and their experience and to ask questions of them: "How did you do it? What does it feel like?" And through being themselves, they became great world teachers. It is not a matter of external pressure. It is a matter of internal surrender, of allowing.

You will walk through fear and you will see that it is an illusion that has no power over you. You will walk through doubt and you will see it is an old thoughtform that is not yours any longer. And when the channel within you is open to the Source, there is never a feeling of lack at any level of your existence. If the channel is open there is always abundance, there is always enough love. There is always enough wisdom, clarity, energy.

So how do you like my little pep talk? Do you think I have a future in coaching? We cannot play the game for you; we can only stand on the sidelines and cheer you on. We can pass on the plays to you, but it is up to you to execute. Execute these plays and you execute the ego! It is time for you to wholeheartedly accept your own worthiness. Recognize that all beliefs of limitation you have carried about yourself, all guilt that you have carried, all self-doubt, these are not yours. These are thoughtforms that are alien to you. They are not real. It is time to cleanse yourself and purify yourselves of these old energies and allow the process of transformation to continue.

So my dear ones, I would like to share with you more of energy and more blessings. I would also like to offer you the opportunity to ask questions. So now is your chance. Please, how may I serve you?

"How can we speed the process?"

Be careful what you ask for my friend, or it may be speeded up so much that you will say, "How can I slow it down?" Perhaps ask that the process proceed at the velocity that you can accept gracefully. Give yourself to meditation consistently, and follow your inner Self, follow your heart. You will be guided to the proper places and teachings and experiences. Just love yourself and open to that. Stop trying to escape from it all. You are missing all the fun! Many would desire to be in your shoes right now. Each day offer yourself to Spirit and ask that your heart be purified. Ask Lord Sananda to grant you the grace of devotion. Ask and you shall receive. And have patience with the progress that you are making. Know that it is occurring as rapidly as you are capable of receiving.

"How is it possible to differentiate when truth is spoken and when partial truth is spoken?"

First of all, understand that truth cannot be spoken. All that can be spoken are reflections of truth, reflections of that light. As some reflections are more pure and brilliant, they will feel to you more like truth. Others may feel more twisted or controlled, or coming from limited belief patterns. There is no perfect expression of truth that can be heard with the ears. The perfect expression of truth can be felt in the heart and with the inner senses. Your discrimination will be enhanced through going within and activating the inner senses. Each of you have systems in place that act to discern what is truth. There is a meter inside of you, like a little bell that rings when you feel the vibration of truth coming through the words. So simply use your feelings and screen out that which is not for you. You will find yourselves being more and more attracted to beings whose speech reflects a higher percentage of truth than to those who indulge in ego projections. Trust your feelings. Know that your experiences exist to teach you lessons of discernment.

"Michael, what is the role of Atlantis and the Atlanteans during this period?"

Are you from a bygone era? Well, get with the present, my friend! What is happening now is far beyond what occurred in Atlantis. There are many beings who experienced Atlantis sitting in this room. Have you learned your lessons, my friends? There were beings in Atlantis who had experienced previous civilizations also. So don't be overly concerned with one particular lifetime or group of lifetimes. Rather, have the perspective of yourself as an *immortal* being who has had many lifetimes and chooses to focus that energy in this time and space continuum you call the "now." You are going to have your hands full in this time. Some of you may be drawing upon Atlantean experiences. Your Higher Self may be trying to remind you of something that you learned, so that perhaps you don't have to learn it over again, or reminding you of something that can help you now.

"Lord Michael, are all beings going to ascend, or will it just be choice? Will there just be some?

The opportunity is offered to all. The opportunity is currently not being accepted by all, but only by a very few. It is our hope that many, many more will accept this opportunity. It has not been etched in stone as to how many will choose to go on into the higher dimensions, or how many will choose to incarnate again in physical realms. But everyone will change. This is the planet of change, and now it is especially true. So be concerned mainly with yourselves. If you will work upon your own ascension, you will do the maximum that you can to assist others by holding that doorway open in your heart, in your words, in the light of your eyes.

"Archangel Michael, how soon should we expect this to happen, the ascension of ourselves and the planet? Does it have anything to do with the approach of this other object coming close to us?

It's already happening, my dear. It's a process, you see? All of these types of phenomena have a role to play, but they are not the cause. The cause is the end of this planetary cycle. What manifests as phenomena are not as important as the energy-feeding that is coming from Source at this time. The universal life circuits are being reconnected, and each being is feeling the effect. The planet is feeling the effect of this increased voltage of light. It will cause choices to be made. It will cause separation and realignment, a separation of those who do not choose to go into the higher dimensions. So there are many possible scenarios of how the universe and the solar system and the planet will react, and what the planet will create for herself in her growth experience. What the universe will allow is very wide open, a panorama of possibilities. It is possible for objects to collide with the Earth. But let the Earth decide what she herself requires. And don't believe everything you read.

Now it's time for our meditation. I would like to ask each of you to relax and breathe. Open yourself to receive this energy transmission. Allow it to be intensified to whatever degree you are capable of receiving. It is an energy which will assist in your unveiling as a divine entity, and in opening you to the awareness of yourself at a deeper level of your being. Just breathe, and see the light within. Know you are surrounded by a beautiful energy field. The angelic beings and the Ascended Masters are here with us, blending their energies together.

I would like to ask you to visualize, in the center of our circle, a beautiful ball of light, a white and blue radiance. Simply open yourself and allow that energy to penetrate your heart. Allow the radiant ball of light to expand and fill this entire room. Allow the energies of purification and healing to flow around you and through you. Relax yourselves and just be in that light for a few moments.

So, my beloved ones, thank you for your attention this evening, for your focus. You may remain in meditation for a while longer. The energies will remain with you. I encourage each of you to open your hearts to these energies that are coming through now in your lives. They will purify you, align you, and remove the veils. Open yourselves to that which longs to come through you from Spirit, whatever it might be. Enjoy your experience. Enjoy the aspects and the multidimensional nature of your existence here. Enjoy the physical. Enjoy the emotional and the spiritual. Enjoy your minds. Let the light of Spirit flow through you, through every part of you. Don't withhold it from yourself. Don't judge yourself unworthy, but open and know that every cell of your beings, every experience within you, is one with that Source. And allow, just allow the process to continue. With focus and patience, you are bound for glory. Thank you for your attention. I love you all so much. Call upon me for assistance and I am yours. Goodnight.

CHAPTER FOUR

DIVINE LOVE

⟪ Sananda ⟫

Good evening to you all. This is Sananda. How are all my pals this evening? You are my pals, you know, among other things. Sometimes I think you are my patients! Just relax yourselves. If you are new to our gatherings, make yourself at home. Focus on your breathing. Relax, and let me do all the work. You have had enough work for the day, the week, and for an entire lifetime, I would presume. Let's take a little holiday together this evening. Just allow yourselves to relax. I come to you on a ray of divine love this evening, with love and compassion in my being for each and every one of you. As I bring through my energies, I wish to allow each of you to experience my presence in a deep and meaningful way. In doing so, you will experience yourself in a deeper way, for we will be communicating from the point where we are one, from the essence.

Love balances all. Love is the essential stuff of creation. Love looks like light. What it feels like is only known experientially. What it is, perhaps, is the heart and soul of the Creator, who exists in all dimensions, in all particles of existence, and in the space between the particles. This love energy of the Creator manifests itself multidimensionally in many worlds, in many species and creations. It manifests itself uniquely in each individual being with consciousness. That's where you come in. You could say that the creation is nothing more than an attempt by Source, by the Creator, to know itself. And the purpose is experience. Through all of your senses the Creator witnesses the creation.

Just so you don't take things too seriously this evening, you see, that love essence, that energy, *enjoys* its experience — as you are meant to enjoy *your* experience: with humor, with a carefree attitude. When you have connection with oneness, with Source, the process of ego-identification begins to dissolve. When that ego-identification dissolves, you have God-realization, the elimination of separateness. This is a step on your path. It is a point beyond preference for good over evil, beyond preference for one experience over another. It is a point of surrender and delight.

Through experiencing your life, consciousness creates a process of growth. Growth is nothing more than the accumulation of experience and learning from that experience. It is the expansion of consciousness. Within a human being, all of the fundamental and necessary building blocks of consciousness — all of the tools that are required — exist, making it possible to go directly into union with Source. You could say that animals are also one with the Creator, that they have consciousness to a certain degree. But the human form in this world is called the crown of creation, for only in that form do you have all of the tools necessary, do you have access to the higher God-Self, that shining path that leads directly to union.

The love that you feel in your life at this point, though it may be rather profound at times, is very small compared to where you are heading. In fact, until a being is surrendered entirely to Spirit, to Source, it is not possible to experience the full manifestation of that divine love. It is too powerful. It is too expansive. Only when a being is fully prepared to handle that much love and grace can that union occur. This is why it has been referred to as a spiritual path, you see. Ultimately you are all one with the Creator in each moment. There is nothing left to do and nowhere else to go. Yet in your practical, pragmatic, day-to-day consciousness, there is still a tendency toward the experience of separateness and limitation. There is still a longing for completion. And every Master who has ever walked this Earth has taught this path to completion. It doesn't matter to us whether you walk this path as a scholar full of intellectual ideas, as an innocent childlike being, or whatever your predilection, yet you must walk this path. It is the evolutionary spiral of consciousness. You are spiralling upward.

There are ways and means that you can utilize to enhance your progress and your enjoyment of the process of growth, in effect to achieve greater and greater liberation of spirit and consciousness. And of course we have outlined this many times in our discourses. Your meditation practice is all important. To still the mind so that you can feel your spirit is essential, for it is a path of experience, not a path of intellectual understanding alone. In meditation, the mind is quiet. The inner senses are activated. The external senses are diminished. For every external sense a human being has, there is a corresponding internal sense. The external senses are used to experience the external world. They make it possible for you to function as a physical being. To become a Master, it is necessary to balance these outer senses through utilization of the inner senses. Otherwise you are living only a partial existence. The grace that is flowing through at this time, for this world, is enhancing your ability to experience with the inner senses, the worlds of Spirit. It is your destiny to attain communication with and consciousness of who you are at higher-dimensional frequencies of manifestation. If you think you are only a physical being, you might as well be walking on four legs with a thick fur coat! Unfortunately, this is the situation of many on this world. Yet it is all part of the process. To you who are walking on two legs, congratulations! You have access to higher-dimensional awareness that will balance you and complete your union, removing the veils you have carried for so many lifetimes.

When you have achieved a certain level of enlightenment, or realization, many opportunities are opened to you, and you are aware of these choices. Until you attain a certain degree of consciousness, there remains a feeling that you have very few choices, that you are limited, that you are stuck here. As you become aware of your infinite aspect, the solidity of the external reality becomes more dreamlike. You realize you are living in consciousness, *as* consciousness, with the power to create, the power to change, the power to access many higher-dimensional energies for your own pleasure and enjoyment, for your own peace, safety, and security, and as a divine service to your fellow human beings. In fact, I would say there is very little purpose for many of you to be here but to realize this aspect of service for humanity and for this planet. Why else would you choose to limit yourselves in this way for so many lifetimes, if not to bring humanity into balance and union, by creating a pathway that others might walk behind you?

So I commend each of you for your solidness, for you have been solid. I applaud your efforts. Your ascension experience will grant you the ability to travel more interdimensionally between the different levels of solidness and spirit, allowing you much more freedom. And yet, the path to ascension leads through this very simple and basic humanness. It leads through the doorway of self-love, and through loving the physical nature of the world, of this body, and of all creations. Enjoy that. In loving it, you channel my love, which is the divine love of Source, through you to heal this world. When you criticize, judge, label, categorize, pigeonhole, or any of the other games you are fond of playing in your mind, you are limiting the flow of divine love to all of creation: "This person is worthy of my love; this one is not. This situation reflects divine higher law; this does not." I ask you to go beyond these judgments. Can you walk with an open heart? Can you be an open channel in all situations, without judgment or criticism? Can you understand your role in being in a human body? If you can, you will experience the joy, the bliss of being. It can be accessed in the human form just as it can be accessed from an ascended state. It's the same love, you see. You don't have to wait for it.

Spiritual practice, utilizing the inner senses, will assist you in severing your attachment to external stimulation, satisfaction, security. A being who is unaware of their connection to Source is indeed in a state of anxiety, always wondering how they will be provided for, always wondering where they will find love. Who can give it to them? A being who is in contact with the divine love within, with Source, has no need to go without for satisfaction. Going without from that perspective is simply an enjoyment, a reflection, a radiation. It is not done out of need. It is done out of creativity and self-expression. The balance point is within you, dear ones. It has always been there. Now we are activating and assisting you. You could say all obstacles are being removed to your liberation and ascension. Your role is very simple. It is to love yourselves, to access your spirit by utilizing the inner senses. But to go beyond thinking about it, to actually doing it, is necessary.

It's really a matter of letting go, you see. It is the nature of the mind to be attached. It is the nature of consciousness to be connected to something, to be focused on something. Meditation is a tool. It is not the meaning of life. It is a tool designed to assist you with realizing the meaning of life. Within your own breath is your connection to all that is. It is your source of peace. When you surrender the mind to Spirit, for those few moments or minutes or hours, for those days, for that lifetime, you are making yourself entirely available for maximum growth and experience.

You know, you might as well go for the maximum. I have seen how it works with you. You dole it out a little bit at a time for yourselves. This tends to be the nature of growth: a gradual, step by step process. But know that if you ask for more grace, higher consciousness, and awareness, you will receive it. And you will receive it very quickly and very profoundly. This I offer to each of you, and the many Masters and angels are also at your service. You could say they are holding large bushel baskets full of grace and blessings, waiting for you to ask for them. How do you ask? You ask by demonstrating what is important to you in your lives, not merely by spending thirty seconds a day saying, "Yes, Sananda, please give me the gift of devotion and God-realization," and then going out in your day and becoming a crazy person like everyone else! You could say doing this practice may result ultimately in self-realization, but I don't think you'd like to wait that long! You demonstrate your intention and what is important to you by your practice. Do you take time in your day to focus exclusively on Spirit, to open yourself, to offer yourself in the stillness where your spirit dwells, where it connects with you? This is how we know you are sincere and committed. Without commitment and consistency in your practice, you cannot receive the powerful blessings that we have for you. It would be overwhelming. It would make you dysfunctional. Many beings at this time are reveling in their dysfunctionality. They are claiming great pride in all of their dysfunctional experiences, as a signal that they are evolving. Of course, some of these experiences are unavoidable. And yet you create, by your continued practice, your own pathway. How do you want it to be? Maybe you would just like to be peaceful and happy and enlightened, and experience a graceful transition into your ascended state. Why not? Try it. Your consistent practice will grant you this experience.

On this world at this time, there is so much occurring. From my perspective, things are really hopping. Beings are awakening left and right. Beings are processing old energies of limitation, releasing them, and growing into more of a state of union with Spirit, in preparation for the completion of the ascension that all have been awaiting. This is not occurring only here in this room, or in only several locations — power places, as you call them. It is occurring throughout this planet. It is occurring with beings who are yet unaware of what is truly happening. Yet it is still happening to them. It is necessary that you who have signed on to the service of embodiment and ascension from a physical platform … it is necessary, in the fulfillment of your roles here, to make yourselves available to those who are now beginning this transmutational experience … perhaps as guides, perhaps as brothers and sisters, examples, teachers, but always with humility.

For there is very little time remaining, you could say. There is very little time for beings to choose their alignment and to commit themselves with purpose. For in the accelerating days ahead, all beings will experience the manifestations of their choices, their projections. A being who is thinking for thirty seconds a day that he would like to experience God-realization and ascension, and the other twenty-three hours plus giving himself to materialism, will very likely not have the necessary empowerment to shift as that shift occurs. Those with sincerity, who make the effort that they can make, will be rewarded beyond all expectation. You may enjoy the pleasures of the world. That is what they are there for. But don't let them take you out of balance. They are not the purpose of your life. They are just part of experience and learning.

So much is happening, my dear ones. It would be wonderful if I could, from this perspective and through this channel, sit here and tell you exactly how it will manifest for each of you. But this is not possible, for you are creating it now and in each moment. I can only tell you it will occur. Your ascension is occurring and will occur. In essence, you might say it has already occurred, but you must be beyond time to have this perspective.

There will be many powerful manifestations, purifications, on this planet, as you have already witnessed, as beings reap the rewards of their karma and their choices. You have it in your power to be above the fray, to be above and beyond this, to act as examples that others may witness. Maintain your peace, your joy, in the midst of turmoil. What human beings have grown accustomed to on this world as the normal state of affairs would appear from many other perspectives to be total lunacy! Visitors arriving here from other worlds might say, "These beings are in great distress. I don't know how they can function!" It might look quite horrible to them. And yet human beings have grown accustomed to this. A certain level of horror has come to be expected on the evening news. "Oh look, it's no more horrible than it was yesterday. I guess we're all right." But as you sensitize yourself to Spirit, the experiences of this world can be at times very difficult for you. This is all the more reason for you to maintain your connection with Source, to maintain your spiritual focus and practice so that you can be lifted, so you will not be at the mercy of negative energies.

So, how are you all doing so far this evening? Am I entertaining you well enough? In speaking from my heart, which is all anyone can do, it is my longing and my desire to bring you all into the divine love that I feel, that I have recognized as my essence. It is very challenging to put into language, on these occasions, that which cannot be spoken. Indeed, our communications are growing more and more etheric all the time. So I would like to share with you a bit more, energetically, of these divine waters of love that your hearts and souls are truly thirsting for. But I would also like to offer you the opportunity to ask questions if you desire. I will try to evade them as best I can! If you have concerns you would like me to address, please feel free.

"I have attachment to things. I'm trying not to want things so I can grow beyond them."

First of all, don't perceive this as a problem. Perceive it as part of your spiritual path. It's taking you through a realm of learning in this area. It is a sacred teaching which you are giving yourself. In experiencing this, you automatically dissolve attachment to external sources. For what you are seeking is really to fill that empty space within. If it is relationship you are seeking, you are really seeking more divine love, thinking you will receive it from another person. If you can go direct, you will not be attempting to receive it from another person. You will be complete within yourself. Then your relationships will not be dysfunctional or codependent. Don't view it as a big problem, but give yourself to spiritual practice. Don't chastise yourself for having desires. It is natural. All beings in the physical body have desires. It is nature. There will come a point of release, or realization, of merging. There comes a point where something lets go in you. Then, all is peace and satisfaction. At this point it does not mean there will no longer be desires, but they will be subservient to Spirit, rather than you being subservient to the desires. The nature of human existence is to experience your desires and to learn from them. As I said, it is a world of experience. It is not a pill that I can give you. If it were, you would all be ascended. And someone else would be channeling you! The commitment you give to your meditation practice is your number one focus. Love yourself. Don't chastise yourself. Allow the process to unfold. It is unfolding.

"Lord Sananda, I know that when we ascend we are given choices. At this point, I feel in my heart that I would not want to leave this plane at all, that my ascension is taking place minute by minute and that I will just, in the twinkling of an eye, have a light body and will have learned in that multidimensional state all that I need to know to be a teacher here. Can you speak on that in relationship to going up into the ships and taking additional training and coming back down?"

Yes, this is possible. The shift into the ascended state, if one gives oneself to spiritual practice, can be achieved in this way. It is entirely possible. Yet it is very likely that in that shift, in that final shifting into the ascended state, there will be a need for a time of integration. It will be a little disorienting to your being. There will be a little bit of time necessary to acclimate yourself to what it actually means to be in a light body. So the length of time that is necessary is dependent on the individual. There is no prescribed or necessary step by step path that is right for all. So it is perfectly acceptable to do it in this way. It is a projection which you will most likely manifest. But if you should find yourself, in your ascension experience, spending some time acclimating with members of the Ashtar Command, or with angelic hosts or other beings, then you will just have to surrender to that, my friend. And know that your so-called leaving of the planet in this way will not be detrimental. Everything that occurs from that point on will be exclusively highest wisdom. It is difficult to put these things into words, as you know.

"I was just feeling I had the power and knowledge within to attain the wisdom without having this experience on the ship. But I do fully understand the integration process."

You see, you are integrating now. You are in process right now. There is much talk of evacuation versus ascension. Evacuation may be necessary for those beings who have not reached the completion of their preparation when the final shift is made. If the earth were to open underneath this room this evening, you could say there would likely be an evacuation that would take place. Some of you perhaps would be experiencing, along with your evacuation, the experience of ascension. Others would first need to complete their training with the Ashtar Command. Ultimately, the destination is the same.

"I'm a visitor from England. We have information in England that a group of Australians says the first wave

of ascension has begun, and that they have instructions as to how to proceed. I'd be interested in your comments about this."

There is much confusion. There are many beings who have had certain spiritual experiences and who are claiming they have ascended. The ascension is not something that a being will be able to remain in their physical form and claim that they are now an Ascended Master. An Ascended Master does not claim anything. Indeed, an Ascended Master does not return to the physical in the same way. They may materialize the light body on the physical plane, but it is no longer the same physical body. There are beings who are making claims that are based on these experiences, but they have not completed the true ascension. The moment of the full attainment of the light body is the essential moment, the true ascension. Though you may experience your body transmuting and changing, when *that* shift occurs, believe me, you will know it. It is very dramatic. No matter how much preparation in a gradual way you undertake, that moment of ascension is a dramatic experience. So perhaps, in this case it is only a matter of semantics. Everyone seems to have their own belief structure around this experience. What is important to me is that you are indeed surrendering to Spirit and allowing my divine love to assist you in that completion. Don't be so caught up in semantics, or in trying to understand it intellectually. Ultimately, you will be as little children in that moment. Each experience is sacred. Whatever a being is experiencing is their perspective, their reality. And that is their grounds for learning.

"I have two children. Is there a way to present ascension to children so they will feel safe?"

I suggest you follow a "hands off" policy. In other words, you don't need to tell them anything about it. Just practice. Give yourself to your spiritual practice.

"My daughter is afraid of death and afraid that I'm going to die. I want to be able to comfort her."

Comfort her by telling her that nothing dies, and just love her. It is a natural fear of children. There is no need to complicate matters by talking about evacuation into spaceships. You see, the children are prepared for this. They knew it was coming when they incarnated here. So when it occurs, if it occurs in that way, they will be prepared. Just be natural and loving. If there are questions asked, go within. Ask me to assist you to bring through an answer that is comforting, and I will assist you. If no questions are asked, simply love unconditionally. And play a lot of games! You are not alone. None of you are alone. I am here to assist you in your challenges. And not myself alone, but many Masters are with you.

"I feel I've been on a special path for quite some time now, and one of the things I've tried to do is to 'Seek ye first the kingdom of heaven and all else will be known to you.'"

Who said that? That was a very wise remark! I'll have to try that sometime.

"I've had great spiritual insights, and I've also had great materialistic manifestations like inventions, books, and great ideas that could bring me a lot of money. But I don't feel I've quite got the kingdom of heaven within me yet. What would you do when the next step is either materialistic for money or trying to find the kingdom?"

It's not either/or. There is a tendency in your mind to perceive dualities of light and darkness, good and evil, material and spiritual. Really, money is spiritual also. It depends upon the purposes you use it for. So if you have a gift, an ability to make money, perhaps you could share it with some of these other poor souls here! Do what is necessary to sustain your life. Do what is exciting to you. Give yourself to spiritual practice, and don't feel that you are off your path if you are doing something that is having material or financial benefits. That also is a spiritual growth experience. Offer yourself to Spirit and follow your heart. Let your mind be inspired with whatever inventions or ways and means you utilize to exist in this world. You will be doing fine. Just enjoy it as play. It will not prevent you from your ascension. It will not keep you from the kingdom. Only the belief that it will keep you from the kingdom will keep you from the kingdom.

"Why do you not materialize to us?"

There is always divine highest wisdom and purpose behind the way that Spirit works. I have materialized for many beings. It was highest wisdom within the context of their growth that this experience be given to them. If it has not been given to you as of yet, it can possibly occur for you, but only if it is highest wisdom. You came to this arena of activity as a challenge of spiritual attainment, not only as a servant of the light, but to boost your own spiritual growth as well. So there is a lesson within this for you. There is a lesson in faith, trust, discrimination … many, many more lessons and more benefits for each of you. Were we to materialize for you, it would not alter the facts. It would not alter the need for you yourself to go within and to attain self-realization and mastery. I am here with you now and always.

"If a person has died and dropped this body and has moved on to the fourth dimension, what part does that being have in the ascension?

It is an individual experience. It depends upon the evolvement, the attainment of that individual. If a being goes into a heavenly state in the fourth dimension, when the cycle is completed the heavens of the fourth dimension will open and those beings will also have the opportunity of going into the ascended state from there. There are beings of the fourth dimension that are serving those in embodiment as guides. Others are simply enjoying the fruits of heaven, waiting for their number to be called. There are other experiences in the fourth dimension also, many heavens and hells, so it is an individual matter, you see. Everyone reaps the rewards of their attainment, of their choices. Many will attain to their ascension from that which you might refer to as the death state, not in bodies.

"Regarding people who channel Ashtar, there is a person _____. Does she channel Ashtar? Are there many beings channeling Ashtar?

More and more all the time. Yes, she channels Ashtar. This does not mean that every transmission from a being who channels Ashtar is a one hundred percent clear and perfect transmission from Ashtar, you see? The bulk of her transmissions are clear and pure. As with all channels, there is no such thing as a perfectly one hundred percent clear transmission. It is impossible. There is too much resistance. There is resistance within the channels and within the energy fields of the Earth plane. So there is always an opportunity for confusion. That is where your discrimination comes in. If you can trust your hearts to tell you what is truth, what is acceptable and beneficial for you as an individual, you are better off. There are many channeling not as clearly. There are some channeling quite clearly. Ashtar through one channel may sound slightly different than through another. Channeling is something for you to engage in if your Higher Self draws you into that experience. If in giving yourself to spiritual growth you feel yourself contacted by Ascended Masters, if you feel the desire and the longing within yourself to speak their words and to share in this way, the doors are open, my friends. If it is not highest wisdom, or not in your destiny path to do this, you will find other ways to channel your divinity. Even a message that begins with clarity can come through a channel and be filtered in such a way that it is colored a little bit. Does this help you, my friend? It doesn't do much good to be overly wrapped up in ideas and words, anyway. Where you are going you'll have no need for that type of communication. This channel once wrote a song, and there was a line in the song that said

"Language is the devil's daughter." A very inspired line, don't you think? Now we are embarrassing him! If you were a being intent on creating confusion in the earthly sphere, what better way to do it than to create language? "Let's rob those beings of their telepathic abilities. Let's make them use language instead. Then to top it off, we'll create thousands and thousands of languages. That ought to keep them guessing for a few million years!"

"I have a question about integration, I wonder if you have some suggestions to help us integrate. I'm having a hard time focusing on things like making a car payment and ascending at the same time. All I want to do is sit in meditation and I'm finding it sort of repugnant to do my normal survival game. Have you got any suggestions?

It's not easy, is it? How long has it been since you were informed of the possibility of the ascension experience?

"Maybe two months, but I've been preparing for the information for many years."

Yes, preparing and finally hearing. There is quite a bit of excitement and enthusiasm when you first come in contact with this reality. The first months are the hardest to integrate. Some in this room have perhaps been aware of this for a great deal longer. It becomes much easier with time to continue your earthly lives and to realize that there are no discrepancies between fulfilling your earthly responsibilities and fulfilling your Earth mission. If you attempt to bypass your earthly responsibilities, you are in effect bypassing growth experiences that you have given yourself to strengthen yourself, to learn, and to process in a way that you will be prepared to take on your mission. So you need to integrate, in order to integrate your mission. If it was a matter of meditating only, we could get a few jumbo jets and fly you all together to India. There are a lot of vacant caves now. For centuries and centuries human beings have been carving meditation caves. But your path is much more involved than simply withdrawing inwardly.

You withdraw inwardly for guidance, for sustenance, for nourishment, grace, light, for the process of growth. But you then must open externally and share and touch the beings of the Earth, and touch your blessed automobile. It will get easier for you, my dear. Sometimes you just have to jump around and shake. The energy within you just wants to move. Sometimes you feel like you're just going to explode. You've got to get grounded. Keep your feet on the ground. Jump around, scream and shout, maybe go dancing. Express yourselves, your artistic creations, whatever you do. It is not time to hold it all in; it is time to let it all out. Just make sure what you are letting out is coming from your Higher Self. That's the trick.

> *"Over the years, I've developed an attitude of respecting Mother Earth and healing her, but I'm a little confused. If the Earth is going to ascend to the fifth-dimensional state also, why should we bother sending our energy to her now?*

Just as you are individually in a process of preparing for ascension, so it is with the Earth. Out of love for her, out of compassion and gratitude for the support that this beautiful heavenly being has given to you in your many incarnations, it is a simple matter of love and compassion to assist by sending love to the Earth. This will ease the transition that she is making. You know, you can have an effect upon earthquakes when you give yourself to the light. They can be much less traumatic, much less intense. So the birth traumas that the Earth is going through can be lessened, can be a more graceful and more enjoyable experience for her also. View her as a being who is being re-birthed, and view yourselves perhaps as midwives. It is simply a matter of love. When you feel a lot of love, you just share it. So share it with the Earth and share it with your fellow beings. If you are radiating love, it is going into the Earth. This is ultimately the healing energy that she requires. And she is doing fine in her transformation, by the way.

"In some of your earlier transmissions, you mentioned the children of various ages — that they would ascend and be taken care of. What is the maturation age for them to be taken up? What about the ones that are eighteen to twenty-three years of age?

First of all, the background awareness and understanding is that all beings will attain to their perfect state of evolution during this transformation. It is not for you to look at others and say, "Oh, they are doomed to hell. What can I do to save them, those poor souls?" Those beings who end up in that sort of an experience will find themselves quite at home there. They will feel, "How wonderful, I've finally gotten rid of all those crazy lightworkers! I've got them out of my hair. Now I can do what I want!" So it is for you to understand that within the completion of this cycle, all of these details will be taken care of with great love and great compassion and great mercy. Many of those who might be considered borderline cases will be allowed in the door.

Concerning the children: at a certain point, a being takes on responsibility for their own decisions and their own lives. This is when they take on their adulthood. This point is not easily defined, as it varies with each individual being. For some it could be eighteen years of age, for some it could be a little older, for some it could be a little younger. If you have children, I would say the chances that they are Starseeds is very high, and that if they are not open to receiving this information concerning ascension, they will be. Maybe you will have to ascend and come back and remind them. It may be that they will ascend at the same time as you. Know that they will catch the wave that they are meant to catch, that they are able to catch. You cannot cheat an individual human being out of the growth experiences that their Higher Self has programmed for them. It is not highest wisdom, nor is it compassion to try to do this. You can't grab on to someone as you are about to ascend, and take them with you. They would feel quite out of place where you are going if it were not their time, you see? So all these things occur with highest wisdom, according to proper timing.

It is for you to detach from your own programs. Many of you have mental programs about how you will serve the Earth and save humanity from itself. Your plans also need to be surrendered to what is highest wisdom. Give yourself to Spirit and let Spirit move and transform you. This is what you are here to do. In doing this you are serving humanity with the utmost compassion and power that you can. If you are on the ascension path, you would be surprised at the effect that you have on others even without speaking, simply by looking in their eyes or being in the same vicinity as they are. The energy of your heart will open their hearts. You don't need to have a program or an agenda. Give up your agendas. Be as little children. It's much more simple that way. If you find yourself guided and inspired or moved to speak to someone, or to say something to someone concerning the ascension, know that it is probably highest wisdom and their time to hear about it. If not, love silently. You will have your hands full dealing with human beings and assisting them. Don't be afraid to take some time for yourself now. Give yourself to the process and to the joy of the experience. It is like feeding your own batteries. You will all be utilized, believe me. Give yourself to this process.

I love you all so much. I hope you will not take my humor in the wrong way. I tease you and play with you because you are as family to me, as my brothers and sisters. And I see you as ones having already realized and transcended these questions and problems, for ultimately you are. So if I take them less seriously than you do, I must beg your pardon.

Let us have a few moments of meditation. I would like to bring through some divine love energy for you this evening. Just relax and breathe. Allow my presence to enter your being in whatever way feels appropriate to you. Whatever way you feel it, it is me. You are surrounded with light and protection. I will work individually with each of you in this moment. I will work with opening your heart, magnifying your inner compassion, your inner devotion, your divine love. This will act as a balancing and healing for you in all of your experiences.

So, my dear ones, it is time for me to call it a night. I will remain with you, of course, as you desire, in your meditation. I will remain with you, as I have always, throughout your existence. Again, I remind you to have consistency in your spiritual practice. Don't take it all too seriously, but give yourself to the enjoyment of your lives. And trust. Always trust. Let go to the spirit that is within you. Give yourself to the inner senses in meditation, to the breath, to the inner light, to the celestial harmonies that are singing. Call upon me in your practice and I will assist. Love one another. And have compassion in your hearts for all beings of this planet, without judgement or criticism. Open to love always. Let the divine love that you are channel through you. Let it pour through as powerfully or as gently as Spirit dictates in each moment. Have no fear. You are in good hands. Good evening.

CHAPTER FIVE

CREATING THE LIFE YOU WANT

⇝ St. Germain ⇜

Good evening, this is St. Germain. I am here with all of my love and respect for each of you. I have some very practical matters to discuss with you this evening.

So how are you enjoying your lives so far? You know, it is commonly believed by most of our students that we concern ourselves exclusively with spiritual matters. Tonight I wish to speak with you quite intimately, to stress the fact that we also care for you in very human ways, and that it is of concern to us how you are enjoying your lives. You see, those of you who have committed yourselves to spiritual growth, we have taken you under our wings. All of your concerns and experiences are our concerns, and indeed our experiences, as we are connected. We see through your eyes. We experience through your senses. We sense your emotions. And we love you so deeply, as we know that you feel the same for us.

So, tonight I would like to share with you some perspectives in the areas of self-mastery and manifestation. I would like to lend you my support and assistance in creating the life that you desire. I know if many of you had your way you would be viewing the Earth from a higher perspective right now! But these wishes are far outweighed by a deeper wisdom, as your destiny paths as unfolding Masters far outweigh the desire for immediate evacuation.

Perhaps you are beginning to realize more and more every day, as you give yourself to your spiritual practice, the reason why you are here. And maybe you are beginning to witness the benefits the Earth is receiving by your presence. Sometimes this is not apparent to you. Other times it may be. But while you are here in service to the divine, as we all are, it is important that you know you are also here to enjoy yourselves. Many times you have certain beliefs about service that you might equate with self-sacrifice, with "doing without," in some ways. But an important part of self-mastery involves dissolving this illusion once and for all. What do Masters do but enjoy themselves? What do Masters do but take delight in the many wonders of the manifested creation, in all of the interdimensional interactions that they can experience? It is truly a giant smorgasbord, as they say. So tonight, I come most humbly to assist you in manifesting that which is your heart's desire. Perhaps we can shed some light on your lives and give you a new perspective. Perhaps a few "light bulbs" will go on in your heads and in your hearts. So relax with me, and breathe, and let us share these moments together.

It is all sacred, you know. It is the nature of your mind to always be thinking that the grass is greener on the other side of the mountain. It is the nature of the ego-mind to think this way: "Well, I am doing all right now, but in the future I will be doing much better," or, "When I have attained my ascension I will be doing much better." You are here in this moment to bring mastery into full manifestation, to realize your oneness in each moment, no matter what dimension you find yourself living in. For you will be granted many assignments. You may find yourselves in other times and in other dimensional manifestations and situations, also to serve. It behooves you each to learn the essential, unchanging secret of life in this moment.

So how do you create the life that you want? First of all, are you open to the possibility that what your heart desires is meant to be yours — that all of your needs are meant to be fulfilled, that you are meant to have a life of abundance and joy at every level of your being, from the highest dimensions of Spirit all the way through to your third-dimensional embodiment? At every level of your existence you are meant to be fulfilled, expressing the joy of life. Truly, joy is the essence of life. You could say the problems come in because you tend to create knots in the flow of life. You tend to buy into many limiting beliefs, old outmoded patterns of belief and behavior. Yet here, on this planet of the fallen angels, is an excellent opportunity to learn mastery.

Look at your life, everything about it on every level. Are you satisfied? Are you happy? Are you fulfilled? For you see, here in the Earth school you learn the lessons of mastery that are required in order for you to progress into the next dimensional experience. And that which you believe, that which you speak, that which you project from your thoughts and emotions, manifests in the third-dimensional realm all around you. This is what you call your life. Look at your creations. Pretty amazing, isn't it? I think if there were no Earth school, it would be necessary to create one, simply as an incredible opportunity to learn the laws of manifestation at this level.

Let's use another example. Your higher consciousness, the God-presence within you, is like a clear white light projecting into the world of form through the colored lenses and patterns of your beliefs. You could say it is like shining a clear light through a movie film. And what you see on the screen of manifestation are the projections and creations of those beliefs that you have run through your projectors. So, although at times you may find yourself projecting and experiencing something not altogether positive, surely it is a perfect teaching for you. And each human being receives the perfect teachings for them, based upon their own projections and creations. There are an infinite number of possibilities, many of which are manifested now on this world. Each individual human being is a projector of Spirit into third-dimensional manifestation. Each individual human being channels their own life into manifestation. All of the previous programming they have received and accepted as reality is there, surrounding them, animated, alive, staring back at them from the screen of their own creations. Truly awesome, isn't it?

You see, the Creator, as this energy of light, is truly flexible. And this light is your servant as well as your creator. Any experience that you desire to manifest for your own learning, this energy is more than happy to accommodate that manifestation. It's easier to speak of it in physical terms, isn't it? We could go on about other dimensions, into fourth-dimensional feelings and emotions and psychic experiences, and all these same principals will still apply. But for now, let's stay within the physical realm for our examples. Such as what kind of automobile you choose to drive, if any. What kind of home you choose to live in, if any. What your level of prosperity and abundance is. What your interaction is with other human beings. The grace with which you move through change. Are you a dramatist? You are all dramatists to one degree or another. The human drama of your own creations surrounds you and is interacting with you on the stage of your life.

So assuming responsibility for all that you have created is critically important. For without assuming responsibility for your creations, it becomes very difficult to reprogram and restructure your experience. If you view yourself as a victim of forces that are beyond your control, forces that are larger than you, you are disempowering yourself, cutting yourself off from the flow of that power and grace that does create. However, if you can come face to face with the fact that you have co-created your life, your body, and all that you see around you, then you have opened the doorway of transformation. You did not provide the raw materials, but you molded them.

So, responsibility, opening to the possibility that you can have everything that you need — it is important that you know this now. For now the doors of grace and manifestation are wide open. It is very important that you understand the role that each of you plays in the experience of your life. It is very important that there are no victims left here, that there are only creators, or co-creators. For all that you project manifests. And that which you project now manifests more quickly than ever before. There are still some safeguards surrounding you, so that not every one of your thoughts immediately manifests. But things are speeding up. So it becomes important for you, my dear ones, to attain the understanding that you can have a beautiful life even while you are awaiting the completion of the ascension experience. In fact, you will have more and more the experience that you have no need to escape Earth's limitations, for you will have created, even in the midst of what appears to be a chaotic and changing scene, a beautiful oasis called your life. And in this oasis, you will have transcended the fear and negative emotions that attract darkness and those lesser experiences. It is very important that you love yourselves sufficiently to allow yourselves to have these things.

So, at every point within your experience where you feel a less than perfect manifestation, there is a lesson for you. There is a belief that is not in alignment with highest reality, and it is for you to reprogram these beliefs. And those manifestations, in whatever form of limitation they come before you, will continue to come until you complete the reprogramming and release what is necessary. So, as the saying goes, your worst problems are your greatest teachers. This is true. And if you have felt plagued by one or two things in your life that don't seem to be getting much better ... perhaps you have the experience of fear in your life, or an experience of lack of prosperity — it could be anything — that very experience will continue to draw your attention and open you to ways of witnessing the parts of you that need to be released and reprogrammed, until you have a clean slate, until you create only that which you truly desire. How many of you have given yourselves the freedom to create, as an artist might create on a blank canvas, a life? How many of you have even allowed yourselves the freedom of thought to believe that you can create anything that you desire? And how many of you have looked and seen within that which you truly desire? Often times you have such a strong belief that you can't have everything you want that you don't even take the time to explore what is within you that longs to manifest. Your repressed desires are also your great teachers. So you must also acknowledge and be honest with yourselves concerning those areas where you feel less than satisfied.

So, how does it feel to be doomed to lives of joy and happiness? You see, all human beings are like those beautiful little white rats in the laboratory maze. There is only one way out of the maze, though there are many paths to choose from. Sooner or later, the rat will find its way out of the maze. Though there are many choices, there is only one door out of the maze into the next level of evolvement. And that is your path. In order to find that door, you must make all of your choices and explore all the experiences that prepare you for self-realization and ascension.

Well, how's that for a serious discussion? I just had to get all that off my chest. Everyone take a few deep breaths. You can wiggle around a little bit if you like. My lecture is complete. They don't call it the "Earth School" for nothing! It is very beautiful, is it not, to sit and share these energies?

In doing so, you are automatically activating and preparing yourselves for the next level of experience. You are doing a great service by gathering together in this way. Indeed, it would be highest wisdom for you to honor yourselves for having the courage and openness to pursue a path so steep, when all around you are going to the beach. You are ones who have chosen to climb the mountain, while many more are simply lying on the beach catching some sun. You are climbing to the peak, to reach the source of those rays.

Having a consistent practice of meditation is so important now. It is important now in the maintenance of your clarity, so that you will have the awareness to know that you are choosing your experiences, that you have the ability to co-create your life. If you do not have clarity and peace and the ability to contact your Higher Self, you may have the experience that your life is getting away from you, that it is like a runaway train. When your life is like a runaway train, you find yourself fulfilling obligation after obligation, waiting for a time when you can have a moment for yourself, but always postponing that moment for some reason or another. How many of you feel this feeling from time to time: that things are getting away from you, that you are fulfilling everyone's needs but your own? And you might say to yourself, "Well, after I have been a good person and fulfilled all my obligations, I will be rewarded by having some time for myself. Then I can meditate and fulfill the needs of my soul." It's quite a juggling act, isn't it!

I am here to tell you that it is time for you to live your own lives with strength and courage. Experience your own projections rather than the projections you have taken on secondhand from others. When you allow projections from external sources of any kind to manipulate your consciousness, you lose clarity about what is important to you. And your life does become that runaway train, and you feel you can't find the brakes. You might even find yourselves having to crash once in a while in order to slow down and experience some peace. So have the honesty within yourselves to look at your lives to see the creations that you participate in. If they are not creations that you enjoy, why do you continue? Or if there are other creations that you would enjoy but you are putting off, why do you put them off? You are now empowered to manifest fully, to express your spirits as creatively as you dare. That is the challenge before you. It is yours to accept. The only limits to your self-expression and abundance, love and joy, are those that you accept into your awareness. It is also very beneficial if you don't care what anyone else thinks, by the way. If you worry about what everyone is thinking of you, then you will find yourself living everyone else's life but your own. What do *you* care about? What do *you* want? It doesn't matter if it's what another person would think is valuable. Do you have a strong desire to retreat to a mountain hideaway and write a novel? Does your mind tell you that it's impossible, or that there is no money in that? And so you might let your spirit go unfulfilled, that portion of your Self that longs to express in that way.

You see, the desires of your heart truly are God's will in action in this world. There are also desires of other kinds coming through the ego-self, that perhaps manifest as lesser experiences. Ultimately they are from the same source. They are only being filtered through more density. In other words, a being who has a desire to have one thousand sexual interactions per year truly is essentially having a desire to experience more love, but they are projecting it through more dense filters. But if you will track those desires back to their source, you will find that originally they are pure. All desires spring from the essential longing to know God.

So when you surrender to God's will, you are doomed to fulfill every longing of your soul. Yes, it's a rough life, but you just have to go through with it! So be a little more spontaneous and a little more honest in the way you view your lives. Have courage and give yourself permission to be a little bit more selfish sometimes, and see where that leads you. Generally it leads you into expressing unfulfilled manifestations of God's will. Won't that be wonderful? The world that you live in is made up of millions of beings who have come to the belief that what they desire is not God's will, and so they suppress their desires and live by other people's rules. A radical positive alteration in the state of your consciousness will affect others also. Just as you have been inspired by the lives of others, others will be inspired by your lives. Then you will have to deal with that! So in these wonderful times my friends, when all things are coming to a head here, remember what I have spoken of this evening. Allow yourselves to experience the joy, abundance, and love that you require.

You are here to turn the tide. The way that you do this is by refusing to participate in old patterns any longer. You know the expression, "just say no." Well, there are a lot more drugs out there than you might have been led to believe. Every time you accept another's reality over your own, you are taking a drug. So just say no. Dare to be different. And you can do this in your own quiet ways. It doesn't matter how you do this, as long as you say no to illusion.

These physical bodies are just the shells of your beings. They are a very small part of what you are. The Creator and his agents call you every day and in every way to go within to inner space, to take the journey that will empower and enlighten you. It is a journey that will result in your fusion with the Higher Self in the ascension experience. Do you have any questions?

"I'm curious to know why the focus has changed from ascension to being fully in the present in this life."

The focus is always on ascension, but in order to ascend you must master your third-dimensional reality. In mastering your life in all aspects, you are preparing yourself and accelerating your ascension path. So there is no discrepancy. Attaining self-mastery and enlightenment through spiritual practice, through assuming responsibility for your creations, is the ascension path. Everything that we share with you goes into the pool of your ascension preparation.

Whenever you gather together in this way, you create a beautiful manifestation of light and protection from the Masters, through your Higher Selves. You create this peaceful center. You see how important it is. We spoke before how your life can feel like a runaway train at times. When you gather together in this way you are lifted to a higher perspective, so that you may transform those areas that are causing you discomfort. You need within you the feeling of sanctuary and safety, for indeed there are many ways to get caught up in fear, and many false ideas to catch you in this life. If you get caught up in the political or emotional levels, your mind can easily become enmeshed in fear and confusion. So allow the drama to play itself out. Know that you have a peaceful seat in your hearts.

No more questions? Let us meditate. Let us create together a beautiful energy, an empowering energy that will take us to a new level of expression, a new level of consciousness, from which we need never leave. Won't that be nice? You see, your meditations can have a great deal of power when you ask for what you desire through your affirmations and prayers. You can be a bit more forceful, you know! So let's just relax and breathe. Tonight we will focus on opening the doors of creativity and abundance and manifestation.

I would like you to visualize a beautiful violet flame surrounding your being, engulfing your being and spreading out to fill this entire room and this circle. In the center of the circle, you can imagine a beautiful fire of the violet flames, especially intense. We are surrounding you with light and protection so you are safe and secure. The violet flames will transmute density, limitation, fear. Open your heart to the experience of peace and love within you. Now I would like to ask you to perform this visualization with me. Envision within your heart center, in your breast, a ball of white light the size of your heart, or slightly larger. Just feel it. Whatever color it appears to you, whatever strength or brilliance. It can be a flickering light or a brilliant light. Whatever it feels like to you, allow that. Take your hands and put them together. Bring them to your breast and envision this ball of light that is your "heart-light" going forth into the palms of your hands. Take it from your breast and into your hands. Now stretch your hands towards the center of the circle, and place this light of yours within the light of the violet flames, where they are most intense. Hold your light there. You may feel your ball of light expanding. You may feel it growing in strength and intensity. You may feel that it is taking on a violet color. It is being purified and cleansed. Now I ask you to retrieve your beautiful ball, now glowing and purified, and place it back within your hearts. You will notice the violet flames diminishing and finally dissolving, taking with them all density and dissolving it. You are again integrated, and hold this purified light within your body.

You may use this technique of offering your heart to the violet flames of God, offering yourself up in the light of God. Truly, this is the essence of your life, the purpose of your life, and the completion of your life in this realm of experience. You may continue to meditate if you wish. It is time for me to be going. I will remain with you in meditation if you desire. Know that we are with you in every moment and in every step that you walk in your Earth missions. It is highest wisdom for you to be here, to

be manifesting and experiencing these powerful transformations. You walk in grace and protection. Go within, so
that you will know this at the deepest level of your being,
and this will be a source of peace to you. I love you all so
much. Goodnight.

CHAPTER SIX

INITIATION RETREAT: PART I

⋑ Sananda ⋐

Good afternoon, dear ones. I thank you for coming this holy day with us, to co-create this energy field that will bring forth a healing for each one of us and for the world. It is a most auspicious time to do so, so I thank you. First of all, I would like to ask that you relax yourselves and be natural. We will be bringing through a great deal of light this day. It will be a healing and an empowerment for you, and an initiation. We will be focusing on meditation practice, spiritual practice. We will do what we can to keep it from being too dull. I would like to bring through my energies to open the heart and to prepare the field for the planting of the seed. As the field is prepared, so the seed will grow and flourish: opening the heart center, relaxing all the physical and emotional bodies, removing your cares, your fears, your doubts.

There are many Masters here. We are working together. We are hoping to assist you to harmonize with the energies that are flowing through at this time, and indeed to merge with that energy which is the very source and essence of life itself. As you are aware, there is an increasing experience within your bodies, within your consciousness, of the rising vibratory rate of the planet that you are walking around on. And while it may be convenient at times to act as if this is not occurring, it is becoming more and more impossible to do so. It is up to you to learn to integrate these energies, in order to have a more gradual and graceful ascent into your next form of existence. It is a matter of harmonics. The call note has sounded, the frequency note. And the beings of the planet, and the planet herself, must attune to that. And as you attune to that note, you find that note is again raised in frequency, and you must once again align and attune with that energy. When you are not in harmony with that energy, you feel discomfort, confusion. Those beings of this world that are not opening to the frequencies of light and love that are flowing through are having experiences that are somewhat different than yours. They are experiencing it as a very difficult time, as chaos and confusion, because of their own disharmony.

The focus of today's gathering is to assist you to harmonize with whatever frequency of energy is currently flowing through, by learning to open and become one with the very essence of that energy. You see, there is a subtle force that is the foundation of all that exists, of all of the energy fields that you find yourself in, including your own bodies. You could say you are awash in energetics. If you stop and consider all of the waves of energy that are bombarding you in each moment here in this world, it's no wonder your receivers get a little overwhelmed at times. There is a Source frequency, a Source vibration, the primordial vibration out of which all creation has manifested itself. We call this God at times. Sometimes we just call it light or energy. It is the spiritual presence that exists in each atom, in each molecule, in each moment, no matter what manifestations are occurring, no matter if beings are aware of it or not. That subtle energy of existence, that is the foundation of all, is always present. No matter if you are a physical being of the Earth plane, a lightworker working on becoming an Ascended Master, or any of the hierarchy of spiritual beings — all have access to that same primordial vibration of God. When St. Germain sits to meditate, he meditates on the same light that you do. He may be a little better at it, he may have fewer distractions — less static — as he has risen to a higher-dimensional manifestation, yet he is meditating on the same energy that you can access. You could say there is no escaping from this divine presence.

Human beings in their disharmony and in their judgments have labeled many experiences as being outside of the realm of God, and yet truly that realm contains all. It is simply a matter of being in harmony, in attunement with it, or not. So today we will be tuning you up (with your acquiescence, of course) and giving you methods — meditation techniques — you can use to access those divine energies of Source that will help you to flow more harmoniously through your growth experiences, so you can anchor yourselves at the depths of your being in that joy and love that you wish to experience. All of the forms of limitation are breaking down at this time, as you are well aware. Those thoughtforms that are not in harmony with the light are breaking down, dissipating, struggling to remain alive, but the light is dissolving them. Just as the light is dissolving those energies that you have held within your physical, emotional, and mental bodies that have caused disharmony. Learning to relax, by tapping into the very source of peace, will allow the cleansing and purification process to be experienced much more enjoyably.

The Kingdom of Heaven, as it has been called, is manifesting and will manifest. It will take the perfect form in every dimension, according to the divine plan. Your responsibility is simply to surrender, to allow, and to assist wherever you feel guided to assist. In order to act truly as lightworkers, as assistants in the unfoldment of the divine plan, it is necessary for you to have an experience of what the divine really is. Otherwise you are networking and sharing and unfolding only your own ideas about what it is. Sometimes they are close, sometimes they are very far off. Chances are it is always much simpler than you are making it out to be. We have noticed that complexity lives in the third and fourth dimensions, and that there is a tendency to believe that the divine, the higher dimensions of existence, must be even more complex. Truly, just the opposite is the case. It must be so simple that a newborn baby can do it. Newborn babies are doing it, have you noticed? A child that is within the womb is experiencing the divine light; it is listening to the celestial harmonies. It is only when that child is thrust out into the third dimension and overwhelmed by more dense energies that they lose the memory of this experience. Well, we are here to restore that memory, my divine babies, by teaching you how to attune yourselves to those energies of love, light, and the celestial harmonies that have never left you. They are always present within you, you see? The light — we don't have to create it, it is simply there. In fact it *is* you. It is only a matter of relaxing your filters and taking the time to experience it inside of you.

So, these energies, this divine essence that manifests within a human body as light, breath, and sound is always present. It is life itself, and the source of life. It is the source of your breath, even when you forget to breathe. It is the foundation upon which you have constructed all of your manifestations and expressions. It is the energy you have taken for granted and used. It is the energy you have prayed for in your moments of confusion and despair. It has never left you. It is only a matter of tuning back into it, of committing yourself to that relationship with the divine presence that exists within you. And with that commitment and focus, the miracle unfolds. In fact, you could say the power and presence of the God-energy is so incredible, the miracle is that humans are *not* feeling it! That is why beings who have attained God-realization, who have experienced the manifestation of so-called miracles, do not look at them as miraculous at all, but only as simple manifestations of universal law.

As you approach the spiritual path, it's like climbing a mountain. At the beginning, you may feel guided by others, by a teacher perhaps. You are made aware of the fact that God-realization is awaiting you at the top of this mountain, and that you are walking along a path, a gradually ascending trail through rocks and trees and waters. At first you are unaware that there is any other path up the mountain. You think, perhaps, in that moment, that you have found the true way. Ask anyone who is a member of a religion and they will tell you they have found the true and only way up the mountain. But as you proceed, as you climb, as you rise above the tree line, you gain a vantage point and see that there are many paths leading up the mountain, and that there are many others trying to scale this same mountain. Then you can see that, indeed, there are many other paths, and perhaps at that point you might wish to choose the trail that seems to be the most direct, that looks the most comfortable for you. Then you continue your climb, through trial and error and exploration, until you reach the beautiful snow line where all is light and beauty, where all trails disappear and there is only the final climb through brilliant snow.

You see, all spiritual paths converge in the light. And all belief systems are left behind when you reach that beautiful snow field of light. Perhaps they have served you, but at a certain point it is time to go beyond conceptions, beyond belief systems, into the direct experience of the light itself. What is it that is at the top of this holy mountain that draws you and magnetizes your soul and your heart? One brief experience of this beautiful energy field, the God-presence, gives meaning to an entire existence, prioritizes your life perfectly, makes your life much more direct and simple. And now that all limitations and thoughtforms are breaking down in this beautiful experience of light, it is very important for each of you to learn to attune to that. If you wish to call yourselves lightworkers, you had better make friends with the light. It is what you are. It is not strange to you, nor is it difficult. But it is necessary that you come face to face with who you are. As it has been said in the scriptures, "Blessed are the pure of heart, for they shall see God." What does that mean, to see God? Does he have a long beard? Oh, perhaps, if he chose to look that way to you. But my experience of that presence is that it is light, and it is a light that is beyond all earthly experiences.

So in order to experience this, many beings are choosing many paths at this time, many ways up the mountain. And all of these are valid. It is whatever is comfortable for you, for all methods can be appropriate at different times. If you open your heart you will be guided to whatever way is highest wisdom for you. But know that all these paths converge in the light, in the direct experience of God. The techniques that we are here to share with you today, and to empower you to practice, are techniques that will lead you directly into the heart of God. They are not meant to supplant any other techniques that are working for you, that you may be enjoying. But when you open your heart, you are guided. And so you have been guided here today, as I am guided to share with you what I am sharing — all magnetized by Spirit.

There is nothing intrinsically sacred about a meditation technique. If planet Earth were in complete harmony with Spirit, as many, many other worlds are, there would be no need to ever sit in meditation. Meditation is, you could say, one of the cures for disharmony. Of course, Ascended Masters and other beings also take time to meditate, to focus their energies in a direct feeding from that Source vibration. But techniques in and of themselves are only the door handles, and there are many doors offered to you at this time, many techniques. Some are deeper than others. Some will serve you for a time until you discard them and go on.

What we wish to discuss and share with you today are techniques which will not desert you, which will carry you through to the heart, to the Source. The only way to know what is behind door number one, number two, or number three is to turn the handle and open it up. Behind the doors that we are offering to open for you this day are energy fields of love and light and divine harmonies emanating directly from Source, from the very source of all that exists. So when you turn that door handle of these meditation techniques, there is so much behind there that you might find the door opening quite powerfully. Many times the grace just floods over you. Sometimes it feels difficult to turn that handle, sometimes easy. We will make it as simple as possible, for it is meant to be simple and direct.

So, after I have finished my segment, the first segment this day, you will be introduced to Serapis, a master initiator. He will not say so himself, so I will say it for him. His work while on Earth was as an initiator in Egypt, within the temples there. His initiations continue, but now are given from higher dimensions. You have all experienced higher-dimensional initiations, either consciously, or unconsciously in your sleep. The more you can experience consciously, the more you will enjoy it, the more safe and secure your path will be. You don't need to feel that you are alone. Look around you, look at all these beings that have gathered here today. You have something in common, you have a thirst, a desire. You have a longing in your hearts to know what is going on here. "What is it all about? What is the purpose of my existence, and how can I fulfill that and be happy in the midst of this crazy world?" Have no doubt, we too view this world as crazy. You are not alone in that. If it does not feel completely harmonious to you, there is good reason. It is because you are more sensitive.

So, harmonizing with your spirit will create an energy field around you that will protect you and help you in many ways. It will help you to manifest that which you require for your third-dimensional existence. If you "Seek first the Kingdom of Heaven within you," all things will be added. So let this be your top priority and see what happens. It is time to come to grips with your existence. What are you doing? What is it that you really want? What are you creating? Are you fooling around with this new age movement, or are you committed to complete realization? The more committed you are, the happier you will become. The longing that exists within each being for completion is fulfilled by aligning with Spirit. The purpose of existence is to know who you are, to know that supreme love and to enjoy that, to share that. That is the meaning, the source of meaning in your lives. Do you wish to become prosperous along the way? No harm done. If you wish to become a yogi, no problem. However you wish to manifest that divinity is perfectly fine. But manifest it you shall, if I have anything to say about it.

So, we have a few more minutes to share together before I must say good-bye. I would like to open the floor to any questions you have. There will be opportunities to ask specific questions about meditation techniques later, but perhaps you have more general questions at this time. If there is any way I can serve you, I will do so.

⟡ ⟐⟐⟐⟐⟐ ⟡

"Sananda, I have a general question in an area that is confusing for me, and that is the area of relationships and sexuality. I would like to know if there is some higher-level perspective that you might share in this whole area. Is there an appropriate attitude and an appropriate perspective to take in this area of relationships and sexuality, and could you perhaps share with us a little bit of — at the higher dimensions — what beings experience in these areas?"

Now you are getting personal! The experience varies depending upon the dimensional octave beings find themselves in. There is always intimacy, but it is refined along the way. So it depends what dimension you are talking about. I think it would be best to focus on where you are. Take it to a deeper level while you are here in physical form, and let the rest unfold naturally. Within this area there have been many, many confusions. It seems that each culture has their own taboos. Which parts of the anatomy are all right to look at, for example. We view all this as foolishness. Whatever is in your heart of love is there to guide you, and relationship is perhaps one of the major ways that human beings create to learn about their God-essence. For in that relationship of intimacy, there is a mirror effect. When you are being selfish you see it right away, reflected back to you. When you are giving love, there is that reflection returning to you. So it is a way of learning. It is a way of learning who you are. It is learning what feels good to you, learning the ways to interact with human beings, learning of love. We do not have guidelines for lightworkers or any human beings about how they should manifest their sexual practices. That is up to you. We have no judgments about that, whether you choose to be celibate or not. It is more important that you are following your own spirit. It is not beneficial to unnaturally repress the sexual drive, but rather to find healthy ways to express it. Yet do not be victimized by that drive. Devote yourself to Spirit and you will be purified of unnecessary attachments in this realm. Your spirit will not immediately take away your desire to express in this way, but adjustments will be made. It is a gradual process, not something you can turn on and off in your mind. It is beyond the mind.

So it is for you to decide in your heart whether you are with the right person for you, or whether it is time to say farewell. This is, to put it bluntly, your problem. We are standing here holding out bushels of love for you. We ask only that you open your heart and receive that. And in the receiving of this higher love all of your relationships will be purified, all will come into alignment and harmony. So don't focus on one small area of imperfection to the point of obsession. Focus on the inner light, and learn to trust your feelings. You don't have to give in to the conventions of the world. Have courage, the courage to follow your heart. Know that your heart leads you always in the right direction. If you are confused, take a break until the confusion passes. Now that was a difficult question!

"Sananda, is there a way of healing my own conscious-ness, of aligning it with what is going on in the other dimensions? Is there some way for me to bring that back to this dimension?"

Yes. Your feelings of being split are somewhat natural to the experience of being a higher-dimensional being in a physical form. It sort of goes with the territory. But the discomfort around this can be greatly eased, the more you can directly access the Source. When you go to the Source, all things are balanced and aligned. It is a very disconcerting process you are all undergoing, the ascension experience, the breakdown of the veils between dimensions. So there are definitely times of discomfort. There are times when your body is saying, "Just stop all of this, it is too intense!" There are times when your emotions are scream-ing, perhaps. All this is part of the path, unfortunately. You are breaking through old limitations. So if you can access Spirit directly, give yourself to a deep practice of meditation, take the time to discipline your mind, to master it, then you will see the results. Your experience may not be all that different at first, but your attachment to the experience and your need to gravitate toward acceptance in one area and rejection of another will be diminished. You will become detached and serene in the midst of changes. Then no matter what dimension you find your-self in, the process will be the same. Learning to grow is what is important, not only learning to be a fifth-dimensional being. For a fifth-dimensional being must grow to become a higher-dimensional being, also. So learn to grow, learn to access the Source, and allow the Source energies to flood your being and purify it. Relinquish all attachment to any particular manifestation, and then one-ness will be the result. In union there is no separation. All pain comes from the illusion of separation. I will help you, dear one. Call upon me.

"Could you comment on the Uranus/Neptune conjunc-tion? People are saying that now it's going to affect our conscious awareness in major ways?"

Yes, it is a time of the breakdown of old disharmonious patterns. All that is not in harmony with Spirit will be tending to dissolve or crumble. It is like focusing the light of Spirit through specific colored glasses. When these planets are in alignment with one another, a third color, or a fourth, or a fifth color or frequency of energy comes through. So it is a very powerful time. It is an enhance-ment of that which has been going on for some time. For each of you it is more and more necessary, as we have said, to learn to access Source, that which does not change, that which is stable, secure, always nurturing. So that as you walk through these changing energy fields flooding your external self, you can have that alignment with Spirit that will keep you strong and happy and peaceful. Then those waves can break around your aura, rather than squashing you. Your auras can be so strong that nothing negative can penetrate. So yes, it is a powerful time. It is part of the play. There is a synchronicity. Even the planets are involved. Their energies are focused upon and through this world in many ways.

"Sananda, to feel confident about your own spirituality, is that a healthy sensation or is that a form of ego grati-fication?"

To feel confident and secure is wonderful. To feel exalted, or that you are above others in your awareness is not so beneficial. It is important that you learn to trust

Spirit, trust that part of you which is beyond ego to guide you. In the process, you will find your ego being dissolved. You will find it at times being confronted. For there is a purification that is taking place. There is no need to be so humble that you are a wallflower. There is no need to be giving your divine power away to the point that you are afraid to express yourself. But express from Spirit. Then the power comes through you in a purified fashion, in a way that is in synchronicity with the divine plan in each moment. When you give yourself to meditation practice regularly, it is like taking a bath in light. All that is impure and dirty will be dissolved, and only that which is true will remain. You will become inspired, but not attached to your inspiration. You will become empowered, but not attached to the manifestation of that power. Your heart will be filled with compassion, and this will be the ruling force in your life. Love yourself always, honor yourself.

"Sananda, I'm finding that when I'm away from people who are on a spiritual path for a certain length of time, I seem to be very affected by the third-dimensional mentality around me. I find it extremely difficult to maintain my higher consciousness. I find it harder to meditate. Can you give me any tips?"

Well, first of all, I would say that it is for you to decide what experiences and relationships are beneficial for you, which are harmonious with your state of awareness. There is nothing wrong with leaving when it is not. It is a matter of self-love. And yet there is also a tendency to seek to withdraw from human interactions because others are not as evolved or are more filled with negative emotions. In this case it is best to have compassion in your heart. Be as one who radiates the peace and light from Source, from your heart, and offer up a prayer that you might assist the evolution of all beings of this world. So, you could look at it as a service to be with beings who are less evolved than you. This is ultimately why you are all here. If you were all here to be only with lightworkers, you wouldn't be here at all! There are many more of us in higher dimensions, you know.

So it is a balance that you must find. I would say to look at your life as a service, as a radiation of love and healing for all sentient beings, as a Bodhisattva would. And yet, when you feel it pulling you down, when you feel it is overwhelming your ability to focus, then perhaps go to another place, or another situation where you can maintain that balance. It is for you to decide what the balance is for you. It is quite natural to have times of exultation and times of depression. Sometimes you feel you've got it wired, that you're never going back into the illusion again. Then two hours later you're screaming. Or maybe someone is screaming at you because you've changed. Perhaps they are upset because you are breaking the contract: "You promised to always be the same as me. We have a relationship, don't we? Aren't we here to support one another?"

So you will find a lot of crackling around the edges in your lives. And you will find yourselves being drawn to the company of truth, such as on this day. Again, try not to be overly attached to one experience over another. If you feel that one is good, and one is bad, you are victimized from the start. You are setting up an experience of separation. There is no separation in truth. But also be pragmatic, be practical. If you find yourself always feeling the dark side in your relationships, in your life, perhaps it is time to love yourself and balance that with some quality time. Make some quality time with your spirit, in ways that are nurturing to you. When your battery is empty, you can't serve. So when your battery is drained, it is time to recharge it. When your battery is charged, that is when you may find yourself face to face with demons. You might even be married to one! "Oh, what have I done? I never saw you in this way, dear. What are those curly horns coming from your head?" But to love all with ultimate compassion, that is the challenge; that is the test.

So take care of yourself, dear one, for you are precious. But know that you are here to serve also, and this is the number one way of serving, to interact with human beings. There are no quick fixes, are there? I would like to give you a cosmic Band-aid, each of you who are asking these questions. But I find myself ripping off the old ones and leaving you bare.

So, dear ones, I thank you for your attention. I thank you for your commitment to being here with us this day. Your price of admission into the next phase and level of your awareness is just that: commitment. And if you will commit yourselves to spiritual practice, you will find the energies that we share with you this day will be very empowering, very uplifting. Know that I am yours to command. Call upon me when you need assistance in your spiritual practice. And in your interactions in every moment, I can also be with you. I am overshadowing you. And I can be with you and within you even more power-fully than I have been. The work you are doing, the work you will do, has been and will be successful. So just enjoy. Good day.

CHAPTER SEVEN

INITIATION RETREAT: PART II

⋘ Serapis Bey ⋙

Good afternoon, dear ones. This is Serapis here with you. My goodness, what a large group! I honor you for your participation in these channelings and presentations this day. We shall do our best to assist each of you with the empowerment that you desire. There is a great joy within my heart in this work. It is an honor to participate in this opening. I have worked with many aspirants, not usually so many at once, but I should be up to the task.

The purpose of meditation is to attain the direct experience of the Creator — in essence, to return home to Source. Meditation opens doorways through which you can perceive the heart of that energy, that magnificent Source, that created the expression that you are, that we all are. The Masters do not approach this work from a foundational belief in separation, for in our experience there is only oneness. But for your benefit we must approach it from a very practical and pragmatic standpoint, one which will assist us in empowering you to actually experience that oneness rather than just knowing it intellectually. It is time to go beyond, beyond intellectual understanding of Spirit, into the direct experience: face to face, heart to heart. For this is the only experience ultimately that will satisfy your longing for home.

The direct experience of Source is beyond the experience of ascension from one dimension to another. The experience of Source directly cuts through all dimensions, as far as your consciousness can go, as far as it is qualified and equipped to go. A being existing in a physical body can experience a fifth or higher dimensional awareness, just as a Master of the fifth dimension can experience the eighth, ninth, tenth (or beyond) dimensions in their spiritual practice. In meditation, the conscious awareness is taken into higher realms — for sustenance, inspiration, and as a vital preparation for the total shifting of a human being into the next higher dimension of existence. What we are sharing with you is both a preparation for your personal ascension, and also an assistance to the planetary energy field. For as you lift your awareness and consciousness, it lifts that of the entire world, and all of the beings of the world.

You have the capacity within you for the direct experience of Source. This is not to be taken lightly, and yet it is not to be viewed with an attitude of overseriousness. It is something that you relax into. The effort required to meditate is more an effort of letting go and relaxing than one of striving. For you are already that which you are seeking to contact. And once you have contacted it, the experience of unity shows you quite clearly that you have never been separate. But again, pragmatically, most of you are experiencing some degree of separation. So we are here to apply the medicine, the cure, to assist you, to give you some handles on infinity. Once you can turn the handle and directly approach the infinite, you can let go of the handle and just go into it. But you need something to hold onto, a little guidance about which way to turn, which way to focus. There are many, many practices that human beings use in the attempt to experience the Source.

We are giving you these simple techniques because they are foundational. They are techniques that Lord Sananda taught to his disciples when he was on Earth as Jesus. And many other Masters have also shared these meditations through the centuries.

This is not to say that you must forget the paths you have been walking or the methods you have been using. We are offering you something to open up to, to experiment with. Some of you will find it to be a new experience. Some of you will find it enhancing the other practices that you engage in. Some of you will find that those other practices may become obsolete. This is for you to decide by your own experience. We only offer with open hearts and with trust that you will at least make the commitment to practice these techniques we are offering. The amount you practice, the focus that you give to it, will decide what your experience is. The more focus you apply, the more you will receive. There is no judgment on our parts. There is no test of success or failure. There is only the sincerity in your heart that will be rewarded.

So, creating a space in your life for Spirit to come through, where there is no distraction, where you are offering yourself to be taken into the highest possible experience you can achieve in that moment — this is what I would call meditation — creating that space, creating that vacuum in your life that is not filled with activities, with thoughts, with plans, dreams, desires, worries, processes, but to create a little holy space, knowing that in the creation of that, anything is possible. In sitting to meditate, I recommend that you call upon your teachers and guides. Call for the manifestation of your mighty I AM Presence to be with you. Ask Archangel Michael and the other Masters to surround you with light and protection, to enclose you in an energy field that is safe and secure from any negative energies. If you will ask for help, your meditations can be one hundred times more powerful. The

Ascended Masters are here, offering you everything that we have to offer. Yet we are not allowed to dump it on you. "Oh look. There is someone walking down the street. Let's dump a load of bliss on them and see what happens!" Usually, there must be a previous request. Try it sometime: "Serapis, I'm going out for a walk right now. If you'd like to dump some bliss on me, please do so." See what happens, especially in your meditation sessions. There is so much static in the air, there is so much chaos. The energy is so dysfunctional on this world that you must request assistance. It is a joint effort between your conscious mind, your subconscious mind, and your mighty I AM Presence, with assistance from angelic guides, Ascended Masters, the Ashtar Command and many, many beings. If you will open yourselves to ask for assistance, there is no limit.

There is no time limit concerning how long you need to practice meditation before you can experience enlightenment. All of that is out the window. All of that is going out the window with religions. You see, part of the restructuring that is occurring now is a breakdown of old ways. We're kicking out the middleman, you could say. Now you can buy direct, direct from Source. Well, actually we're removing some of the earthly middlemen, for we are still here. You might even see our faces in your light meditation: "Someone's in my third eye!" And we're not going away. In the past, the pattern was for beings to go to middlemen — priests, ministers, gurus or other physical teachers — and this served a necessary function in the Piscean age. In the new age, you will ultimately go direct. If you wish to follow or listen to guidance from a physical teacher, that is fine. If you wish to come to channelings such as this, all the better — whatever your heart guides you to. But soon the experience of your God-Self will not be dependent on any external factors, only upon your focus, your commitment, and your devotion. So, if going to external teachings enhances your devotion, by all means do so. But do not believe this is absolutely necessary. That is a pattern that is dissolving. We are more than willing to speak to each of you in your meditations, if that is what you desire: to share direct guidance. Though that is not the sole purpose of meditation, it can be a by-product. The main purpose is, as we have said, to go direct to Source. And going direct to Source will bypass psychic involvements and other fourth-dimensional manifestations that are perhaps side trips for you. Time is running out for side trips. Do you want to take a vacation in the astral plane? You'll find there are many to offer you reservations. But if you wish to go direct to Source, we are here to assist in that connection.

For each individual being there are several ways to interact and to contact Spirit directly. Those who have believed they can't meditate, I ask you to revise your opinion. Perhaps our empowerment will assist you. As I said, meditation is not necessarily one specific practice. It is creating that space, that holy space where Spirit can come in. And each of you have created that in the past or you would not be here today. So you need only to find out what works for you.

∞ BREATH MEDITATION ∞

So, the first technique, the first "God-handle" we would like to share with you is breath meditation. The universe is breathing. All lifeforms in the universe are breathing. You are breathing, whether you are aware of it or not. Something is sustaining you. The breath meditation has been taught by many, many masters for many thousands of years here on this world. It will not desert you, even in your moment of ascension and beyond. Some techniques are good for a certain way on the path, but then you come to the need for a dramatic shift and they are no longer relevant. The methods we share today will remain relevant.

So, one of your handles, one of the ways you can quiet your mind and access your spirit, is simply to focus your concentration on your breathing. You can feel it as it flows naturally through your body in a relaxed way. You can listen to it if you are in a quiet place. You can breathe with your mouth open or closed. When you are being lifted vibrationally, for example, as the channel is lifted before his transmissions, there may be a breathing in through the nose and out through the mouth. This acts to raise your energetic frequency, so that you and your guides can get on the same wavelength. You might find this happening to you as you sit to meditate, as you call on your guides for assistance. You might find them pumping you up a little bit. Whatever is occurring, just flow with that. When your mind wanders, bring it back to the breath. When your mind tells you this is stupid, bring it back to the breath. When it tells you you're wasting time, you've got a lot to do, that's an excellent time to be still and focus.

If you will take time in your day to do this, perhaps on arising and before going to sleep, you will find it becoming a very profound experience — not at all what you might expect. It will reveal things about yourself. All that you see and witness, all that you feel, just allow it to pass through your consciousness. And on the altar of the breath, just lift it up, offer it up. All your processes, your self doubts, your ego — on this altar, you can give it all to your Higher Self and have it transmuted.

As you practice this, you will find yourself going into a deeper and deeper, more and more relaxed breathing. You will find activations of light energy, of celestial sounds. You will go into other levels of awareness, even while you are sitting in your body. You will become aware of your God-presence! You will find out directly how God feels, and you will get to know that. There is no need to re-create the breath or to do fancy yogic techniques. You can experiment with these, but we find that the normal breath was created pretty well, and still functions perfectly to connect one with Spirit.

This technique is the foundation of what we will teach you today. It is, in a way, the most important technique, in that you never have to leave it. You can breathe walking to the door, as you're driving down the street, when you're working. There is no need to ever break contact with the Higher Self. And if you will give yourself some time to do this formal meditation technique, sitting in silence and using this exercise, you will find your concentration becoming so profound. You will find yourself experiencing that divine breath throughout your day. In fact, you will realize that it is your sustenance.

It is difficult to look at inner light while you are driving down the freeway. Well, actually it is very simple, but you might not stay in your lane! But the breath is always with you. It carries you, sustains you. It reflects the breath of the Creator, as the universe expands and contracts in its breathing. So take time each day for this. In your moments when you are walking, talking, functioning, if you feel unclear, if you feel disconnected, just breathe. Take a few moments to just breathe. Call upon your guides for assistance. You have heard this many times in many of our discourses. You will probably hear it in every one from now on!

The mind is very active. The mind is like a genie. There is an old story in which a man was walking along and found a magic lantern. And in polishing the lantern, a genie appeared and said, "Oh, master what do you wish?" And the man said, "Oh, wonderful! Can I have as many wishes as I want?" "Yes, unlimited." "So, give me ten million dollars." And in that moment that he expressed the wish for ten million dollars, within one split second, in a cloud of light, a great pile of money appeared. And there was the genie leaning against the money. "Yes, master. How may I serve you?" "Oh, great! How about a yacht?" Another split second, another manifestation. "How about a mansion?" Poof! "How about a beautiful wife, always pleasant, and a beautiful devotee as well?" Poof! And everything this man could possibly desire was manifested instantly. And instantly the genie would reappear and say, "What do you want me to do now? Just tell me what you want me to do?" Pretty soon the man was going crazy because the genie would not leave him alone. He had run out of desires, and yet the genie was still wanting to create. He was "in his face!" So, finally, the man had an inspiration. He said, "I wish you to create a tall telegraph pole right in the ground here." Poof! "And I wish you to climb up and down this pole until I tell you to stop." And the genie did climb up and down the pole and the man finally had some peace. This is your mind! It is a wonderful servant, but it makes a very poor master. You could say that the breath meditation is like the genie of the mind climbing up and down the pole. You focus the mind on the breath and it is stilled. And in stilling the mind you feel Spirit.

The mind must come to rest in order to experience the deepest levels of Spirit. So in one sense, you could say the breath keeps the mind busy while you are experiencing something deeper than thinking. How many times do you think the same thought over and over again? Wouldn't you think that once would be enough? "Thank you for that piece of information. Now leave me alone!" But it won't leave you alone. It keeps coming back. Obsessive behavior, yes? So the breath technique can keep you from becoming the slave of your mind, a slave to the thought-forms that your mind attracts in this world. You can surrender it all up in the breath. If you can't meditate, just breathe. Don't even think of it as meditation. Go for a walk and breathe. Do some yoga and breathe while you are doing the yoga. In stilling the mind, your spirit will come through and the answers that you have been seeking on the mental plane will come to you directly as inspiration. And you will witness your life from a higher perspective. You will receive higher guidance.

Any questions about breath meditation? Pretty simple, isn't it? I don't expect you to have many, it's so simple. But if you do, now is your chance to ask.

"Is it important to take very deep breaths?"

It is healthy. You'll notice when you are fearful, or are experiencing negative emotions, your breath will stop or become shallow. So in observing the breath, you can also get a handle on your emotional state. It is excellent for stress reduction. Just take some deep breaths before you respond with anger or negativity to a situation. What is that they say? "Take a few deep breaths." See if you can't offer up that reaction and receive guidance toward a more appropriate action or reaction. So in your actual breathing meditation, just allow it to flow. Don't control it. If you wish to take a few deep breaths to begin with, to get yourself centered, that's fine. But ideally it is just a matter of allowing. It will become very deep and relaxed as you relax.

"Serapis, when I get in a really relaxed state, I usually end up falling asleep. Is there something I can do to help that situation, or is it all right to fall asleep?"

If your intention is to fall asleep, it is an excellent way to do so. If your intention is to meditate, then perhaps you could get up and move around and wake yourself up. Go out and stand in the cold air for a few minutes, then come back and try again. Ask your Higher Self and your guides to help you to stay focused. Perhaps you're not getting enough sleep at night. If you do get enough sleep and you meditate in the middle of the day, you will be less likely to fall asleep. There is no set time that you need to do this. If you do it before bed and you fall asleep, that's quite common. If you fall asleep meditating, you will have a very blissful and positive sleep experience. If you have insomnia, just lie there and breathe and see if that does not help you. Many people have this problem; they try to meditate but fall asleep. We will give you some other techniques also, and you can go back and forth between them to help keep yourself interested.

∞ LIGHT MEDITATION ∞

So, light. In order to feel God — what God feels like in the physical form — you breathe. In order to *see* God — what God looks like from inside a physical body — you meditate on light. You are meditating on the same essential energy: it is just using a different sense. Just as you have external senses of feeling, of sight, and of hearing, you also have internal senses. The breath is like your internal sense of feeling. The light is your internal sense of sight. The empowerment we share will assist you in the opening of the higher chakras, which will awaken your awareness of the light. The light is nothing less than the God-presence, the lifeforce that is within you. It is experienced with your eyes closed. When you have attained a certain amount of stillness using the breath meditation, focus your concentration at the sixth chakra, the third eye. Just focus your inner attention there and you will see there is a field of light there. As your mind is quieted, you will find yourself falling into that field of light, or feel it filling your form. It can manifest in many ways, as there are many wonders to be experienced. If you wish to assist your concentration, you can touch one of your fingers to your sixth chakra (the point at the center of your brow, just above the bridge of the nose) to help you to focus. You are not looking with your physical eyes. Your physical eyes are closed and relaxed. It is a matter of focusing your concentration, your awareness. In doing so you may feel the energy lifting. You may feel your awareness being drawn upwards, and the crown of your head being filled with light.

There are many, many experiences possible within this meditation. You can see many wonders. Do not be attached to any specific manifestation, but just look, just give yourself to that. When your mind wanders, refocus. It is a matter of focusing and refocusing until you reach a point of concentration where you can instantly go into the light, and where that light can come through you in healing. As you practice regularly, your experience grows. There is no limit. You will find that the inner dimensions of a human being are much, much more vast than the external ones. So all that you can witness with your external eyes will be as nothing to what you can witness with your inner eye. It is just a matter of going within, of placing your hand on the handle and turning it. Just be with it, and allow. You will feel the opening of your sixth and seventh chakras as you practice this. It will remove the feeling of separation and allow you the realization of your divinity in each moment. But you must practice. Talking about it is not enough. How do you become a lightworker? You work with the light. And then the light works through you. It is very blissful. Have you questions about this? Again, very simple.

∾ SOUND MEDITATION ∾

So, technique number three. Corresponding with your sense of hearing, there is also an internal sense. There is a way to hear the sounds of God, the music of the spheres, the celestial harmonies — these are a few of the ways this has been described. To experience the sound meditation, it is either necessary to be in a very quiet place, or to close off the external hearing, at least at first. After you practice for awhile, you can just go into it. It is always present. The human body has, at the front of the ear, a small piece of cartilage, apparently serving no function. Well, we have a function for it! If you would place your thumb on it and press, with a little practice you will find it makes a perfect seal for your ear. By shutting out all external sound, you will begin to hear the internal sound of consciousness itself, the sounds of God. There are musical expressions that you can experience. There are many, many sounds. Generally, at first you will hear just a ringing sound, a sort of a vibration. By focusing your awareness within, usually toward the right side of your head, with your external hearing closed, you will hear this. We will give you a few moments now to practice this ...

As you listen to the internal sounds, whatever they are for you, you will feel an uplifting within your consciousness, within your body. You will feel your awareness being pulled gently upward, to subtler frequencies of being. Focus on a particular sound, say the most prominent sound, for a time. Then you will begin to be aware of higher-pitched frequencies, other sounds. You will be attracted to these new sounds, and concentrating on them will take you to the next higher vibration. Meditating in this way for a while, you will encounter another and another. In this way you climb the ladder of sound, the ladder of frequencies. And this ladder climbs all the way to the Source. Those of you who are musicians or artists will find it very inspiring. Many have been inspired and have tried to re-create what they have heard on the inner planes with instruments and orchestras. Yet these sounds cannot be duplicated, only imitated.

So this is a very powerful meditation technique. It requires a little practice, but you will be well rewarded. After you have experimented with it for awhile, you will find you are able to experience the celestial music with your ears open, as long as you are in a somewhat peaceful and quiet place. Then you will no longer need to close off your ears. If you wish, you can also use earplugs. These can be very effective. Please feel free to experiment with this. I'm not telling you that this is the only way to do it. I'm only telling you there is a divine orchestra going on inside of you!

These techniques we are sharing have been shared by masters throughout the ages. We didn't just invent them. The reason they have been shared throughout the ages is because they work! The reason they work is because they are direct, simple, and with grace, very powerful. Remember, you are not creating anything that does not already exist. You are only observing, merging with it. As you meditate on the breath, on the light, on the music, you will find these senses awakening in a very gentle way. You will find your physical body feels lighter. You will have many spiritual adventures. You will contact the Masters who are always on hand to assist you. But, you must open the inner doors, the inner door of the heart, of the breath, of the light, of the music. And any one of these techniques we have shared will result, if practiced diligently, in God-realization and ascension. Of course, you will experience a great deal in the process of transformation, but these techniques of meditation will not desert you; they will guide you through all. No matter what dimension you find your body in, you will still have the breath, the divine light, and the celestial music to keep you company. You do not need to surrender these or leave them behind upon your ascension. In that moment of ascension, all will be activated, all will be bliss. So prepare yourselves for the ascension by preparing yourself for the merging, the union with Source, or shall I say, for the pure realization that you have always been one with Source.

So, in your practice, perhaps sit in the morning and evening and meditate. Call upon your guides. Meditate on breath for some time, practice light for some time, practice the sound meditation. It requires some discipline. There is a part of you that will resist entering this energy field within you. That is your ego, your limited mind. It will resist it. It will give you a thousand reasons why you shouldn't do that, why it's a waste of time, or why you can't possibly succeed. But if you can only do it for one moment, it will change you. If you can only breathe for three breaths before you fly off into another thoughtform, it will change you. And by giving yourself to it over and over again, you master the mind — you master the genie — and you come into balance as a fully functional divine being. There are enough robots in the world. It is time for some human beings to come forth. Meditation is the source and essence of all spiritual practice, of all practices you may encounter on your path to ascension.

Well, it doesn't get more simple than that, does it? Have you questions before we embark on the empowerment segment of the channeling? No questions; it's too simple. Why did some people know who Sananda was when he was here as Jesus, and others not? They were open. Many were opened by him and by his disciples, who were his initiators, who shared this empowerment. When the experience is lost, you have religion. When the experience is present, there is no need for religion; there is only perfect divine love and grace.

This essential experience is the only thing you will have to hold on to, as your limiting thoughtforms are dissolved. And yet, if you hold on to this spiritual presence within you, you will be provided for in every way. Your dedication will result in miraculous and wonderful lives for each of you. I know you are already experiencing in many ways what I have been speaking of. But today, I am throwing down the gauntlet to you, challenging you to take it a little deeper. I will leave it at that. Call for assistance in your meditation practice. Ask me to assist you energetically. Again, you can go direct. We can assist you just by your request. As to whether you feel us assisting you … that depends on your sensitivity to Spirit. Meditation enhances your sensitivity to Spirit and answers every question.

So, in the next phase, I and Lady Master Kuan Yin will work with you individually. Again, it is not necessary for everyone to experience the empowerment in this way. It is just a little experiment that we are doing. In a way, it is a completion for these channels, and we will see how it feels to you after we have accomplished it. So just sit and breathe. Just relax and enjoy yourself. This is not a high pressure initiation. It is meant to be an enjoyable experience. We are playing with Spirit here. Whatever you have experienced or will experience this day, and in the future, is solely dependent on what is highest wisdom for you at your level of evolvement. You need to surrender to that. You have to start where you are. Start where you are and pray for assistance, and very soon you will not be where you were anymore. So we will try to perform our little empowerment here very efficiently. We will work only briefly with each of you, but it should be sufficient. Already the magic has been working. I ask you only to sit and breathe. And perhaps you could experiment with the techniques we have shared. Let it be a silent retreat for you for the rest of this segment.

So my dear ones, I thank you for your participation in this little empowerment ceremony. I ask you to commit yourselves to practice the meditations we have described to you. Experiment with this. Give yourself a good chance. Not a fleeting chance, but a good effort. Remember that there is an element of discipline required to attain the ultimate experience. It is less than was required in the past, yet it is there. On behalf of Sananda and Kuan Yin and myself, and all of the Masters who are here, we offer ourselves to you in your spiritual practice. Give yourself to breath, light, music. Go within. Give a portion of your life back to Source, that Source may come and completely open you and create that platform from which the ascension can be completed and that union restored. Follow your hearts. We are with you. Good day.

CHAPTER EIGHT

MISSION UPDATE

⇜ Ashtar & Sananda ⇝

Time to charge up the body. Good evening, this is Ashtar. So here we are, my dear brothers and sisters, my fellow lightworkers. When we gather together in this way, there is much light created. And that light projects in a three hundred and sixty degree arc to all beings, to all dimensions. So tonight let us experience some heavenly discourse and some heavenly healing — for you yourselves, for all those you have placed in your healing circle, for all sentient beings of this planet Earth, and indeed, for all beings watching over planet Earth from on high. All will benefit. Where your hearts are in accord and focused, compassion arises. And compassion is the reason for your embodiment in this physical realm in the first place.

Tonight I would like to share a bit with you concerning the Earth mission, its progress, and perhaps we can serve to clear up some points. Perhaps we can create some more confusion! Where there is language there is undoubtedly confusion, is there not?

You see, it is all light. Everything that you have ever seen, heard, thought, felt in any way, touched, dreamed of

— it is all made of the same substance, ultimately. You can call it light. You can call it essence, whatever you wish. And in that direct experience of essence, there is no confusion. There is no language, nor is there need for language. There is only a direct communication of love and bliss. And yet, in order to reach the children of planet Earth with our messages, it becomes necessary to have translators, to have channeled discourses and these types of projections. So we will do the best that we can, within this limited medium of communication, to share with you in ways that might perhaps refine your awareness, your understanding of the ascension process that is occurring for you individually and for your planet. And to this end I will, after some remarks, open the floor to your questions. Now will be your chance. Beings are always asking the channel, "What's new? What's the latest?"

Several years ago, we brought forth through this one our understanding of the plan for Earth ascension and the ascension and/or evacuation of the Starseeds. From our perspective it seems only yesterday that we did this, yet still there seems to be the need for an update from time to time. I will begin with a few background remarks concerning the historical factors that have led up to this situation you find yourselves in at this moment.

As you know, you are here as light-bearers, having incarnated on this "planet in distress," in order that you might assist in the planetary evolution. In doing so, you accepted the descent into third-dimensional physical form. You accepted the limitations of karma, cause and effect, birth and death. And this is what I mean by compassion. For without the ultimate compassion, you would not have taken this journey, this mission.

Now we find ourselves in this present moment, on the cusp of the new age, on the cusp of the cyclic change, at the time that you all knew would come eventually. You could say you have come here to prepare the planet for just this eventuality, the planetary ascension. And this is what is occurring now. You are all feeling it. You are witnessing the karmic clearings. You are feeling the magnification of your own light bodies, the transmutation of your physical bodies into higher-dimensional forms. Many visitors are calling on you from higher realms, assisting you in every way to open to receive the ascension experience, so that you might return to unity with Source. It was hoped that with sufficient numbers of lightworkers embodying on planet Earth — as much as the darkness had spread and the fallen energies had taken control — that the light that you brought, and the light that we have assisted in focusing, would have been sufficient to restore the Earth to her evolutionary cycle in a gradual and gentle way. Much has been done. And yet, as you have all witnessed, it's not perfect yet, is it? In recent times, with the awareness of the closing of the cycle, and given the great distance consciousness needed to come to achieve this transition, it was deemed necessary by Lord Sananda, in conjunction with the Spiritual Hierarchy, to also create an alternative plan. That is the plan we presented in our initial discourses on the ascension.

At the time that these discourses were given, it appeared probable that the only way that the majority of light-workers could possibly accept the ascension experience would be by direct evacuation, as most of you were quite soundly sleeping. And yet, since that time, we have witnessed, through the propagation of these teachings, (and others that have been given through other messengers) a great shift in the planetary consciousness. That is, the lightworkers have begun truly to awaken and to apply themselves to the spiritual path, to regain the compassion they initially brought into embodiment for all of humanity. The motivation for service has been shining forth so powerfully. The sleepers have awakened. Many have awakened simply on the promise that they would not have to be on planet Earth much longer! Not the purest motivation, and yet we must be honest: it has not been easy for you here. Of this we are most conscious.

In our last state of the mission address, only two short years ago — it seems like this morning to me — we spoke about the ascension waves. We stated that the first waves would probably involve ascension in the traditional sense, in the same way that all beings who have ascended from this planet have experienced it. This does not mean it will not occur in waves; very likely it will. You must bear in mind that the experience of ascension requires discipline, focus, surrender, selfless love for yourself and for all. It has been the focus of all of our discourses to prepare you and to assist you on this path, not so that you might escape your predicament, but so that you might be as examples for others to follow. And you are doing so. You are each on your own unique step on the ladder, and that step is sacred for you. I encourage you to continue your climb, knowing that you will be rewarded, that you are rewarded all along the way. I also call forth that compassion within you that can and does know that where you grow, where you surrender to love, you are healing the hearts of those around you, you are elevating the planetary consciousness.

To put it briefly, ascension is the transcendence of the third-dimensional consciousness and awareness, a process completed with the merging of the physical body with the higher-dimensional body, the Christ body, the light body. This divine marriage takes place in a most powerful event. It is an event which does require a great deal of prior purification and preparation. That is why you are all going through your changes, through your transformations. For a lightworker, for a Starseed, the ultimate destination and result of either ascension or evacuation is the same. For a Starseed evacuated via the Merkabah vehicle, the light vehicle, it is only a short step from there into the ascended state. It is a slightly different process, a slightly different experience, but the result is ultimately the same. This is the spiritual path that you are all on. In whatever way the ascension process is ultimately completed, the light vehicles are involved. The Ashtar Command, the Hierarchy, are involved. You do not ascend into a higher dimension strictly by your own will power, as much as some of you are trying to break down the door, as much as there are those all over the planet putting forth propositions that if you will follow this or that technique, this or that regimen, you can force your way into the experience of ascension. You see, ascension comes only when it is time for you as an individual, only when your physical work is complete. This is something you just have to surrender to. You could say that those of you who have been preparing yourselves for this experience have been camping out on the threshold. Some of you are strictly camping out in the doorway, refusing to even look back at where you came from for fear that this opportunity will dissolve. Indeed, it will not.

Your role is not simply to escape from limitation. Your role is to serve. In service, you enhance your candidacy for the ascension. The ascension occurs for each individual in God's time. All you can do is prepare yourselves and surrender to Spirit, do your service and complete your Earth missions as best you can while you are here, knowing and trusting that this will occur in the perfect moment for you, in the perfect way for you.

Another point which has brought some confusion is the involvement of the so-called ships of the Ashtar Command. First of all, we must use the term ships loosely. You might also use the terms Merkabah, light vehicles, or light ships. Each of you individually have access to your own individual Merkabah, which is a manifestation of your multidimensional God-Self. So we exist in our light bodies, and those vehicles which you have referred to as ships are merely our Merkabah manifestations. It does no harm to call them ships. This is simply the way it is for beings of higher-dimensions working to uplift a physical species.

These aspects of God are most beneficial and necessary, our interdimensional transportation vehicles. Also, we can link them together to form great mother ships. So are they ships, or are they us? They are both! And these light vehicles are always actively involved in assisting a planetary species to make the leap into higher-dimensional forms.

So what about the big question? Everyone wants to know when it's going to happen. I wish I knew! The telepathy banks are constantly choked by beings wondering how long it's going to be before they are released from third-dimensional limitations. That is the number one request. There is, you see, a divine plan in effect here. We are servants of the divine plan. We have been given our direction. Part of our direction has been to inform you of our presence and of our capacity to assist you in your upliftment. This we are doing, along with our many other services. With regards to when this occurs, it will occur in God's time. Surrender your impatience to divine higher will. Surrender your judgements and criticisms of your fellow human beings and help them. Help them by, number one, accessing your own spirit in meditation and in your spiritual practices so that you can be a channel of the light, so that you can go through the process and break through the limiting thoughtforms that hold humanity in enslavement. This is what you are here to do. This is what you are doing. Yet you can always increase your focus. In service to the divine plan, the individual preferences and petty desires are transmuted. Not that they disappear necessarily, but they become secondary to the bliss, to the light, and presence of the mighty God-consciousness flowing through you.

So for those of you who are feeling impatient, give yourself to service. See what happens. In the experience of surrender, you no longer care one way or the other what type of dimensional body you are inhabiting. Truly, from that perspective you are beyond such concerns. This experience is available to you. You will have to apply some discipline. You will have to step out of your comfort zones a bit more, if you wish to manifest this with full intensity. If you wish to experience complete liberation while still in the physical body, the self-realized state, the way is open for you. As we have said before, the spiritual path that leads ultimately to the doorway of the ascension must first pass through the corridor of self-realization.

Which brings us around to the final wave, the final stage in the closing of the cycle for this planet, which will involve the re-shuffling and re-sorting of all of the beings and energies of this world. This will almost undoubtedly require the presence of the Ashtar Command and the Hierarchy in an evacuation mode. But the energies are constantly shifting. Only a few years ago, it seemed that incredible Earth changes would be required to purify the energy field of this planet. So much has been accomplished. Some of these expected catastrophes have not occurred. And yet the purification must continue. It will continue to the degree that is required, and only to that degree. This is another reason for you as lightworkers to channel through your healing energies to the Earth.

The end result of this entire process, which we have discussed many times and in many ways, will be a beautiful shift in the energies of this world. All darkness, all unharmonious beings will be removed to areas where they can be given more time to learn from that expression. The Earth, and those upon the Earth who have grown tired of limitation and separation from Spirit are now taking matters into their own hands. With our assistance, and by the grace of the Creator, the darkness is being dispelled. This dispelling of the darkness takes on many forms. You experience it in your physical bodies individually. The Earth experiences it as Earth changes, all sorts of karmic releases. And this will continue to whatever degree is necessary.

Should you as lightworkers, as ascension candidates, require evacuation, that can be accomplished. Let's say you are living on a fault line! An accurate statement, wouldn't you say? Let's say you are giving yourself to your spiritual practice with sincerity, and yet you have not quite attained to that ultimate experience. Should it be necessary for you to be evacuated in the instance of life threatening Earth changes, this can easily be accomplished. This is not a promise or a guarantee, only a matter of fact. It has occurred, and it likely will occur in future.

There is nothing to fear for those who are giving themselves to light and love. There is nothing to fear. There is only to enjoy the unfoldment. Have a sense of humor about it. I do! And honor yourselves, and your brothers and sisters, for the great sacrifices you have made in coming here, for all that you have withstood, and for the compassion that will carry you forward. Never have so few been so mistreated by so many and responded with such love and compassion! Truly you were the right ones for the job. I ask you to continue in your compassion and love for just a while longer. Don't be concerned with times and dates and possible evacuation. Just enjoy yourselves, enjoy the process. If it is not enjoyable to you, maybe you're not doing it right! There will always be moments when it feels difficult. Don't criticize yourselves. Yet if you live in a constant state of wishing to escape from your state, from your lot as a human being, then you are doing something wrong. You are not seeing the big picture. You are not experiencing the direct presence of the Creator in your bodies, in your beings, which is the icing on the cake of physical existence. Perhaps you are being victimized through using only your outer senses, creating imbalance. Use your inner sense of vision to meditate on the light. Use your inner sense of hearing to meditate on the celestial harmonies, the music of the spheres. Use your inner sense of feeling to meditate on your breathing, to feel the presence that never leaves you, that is the direct link to Source.

It is the same link that we have. You are just a little bit farther down the line. Yet your access is just a valid as ours. We are all traveling — via that direct link to Source — on a great evolutionary spiral.

So, as I said, I will open the floor to your questions. If you have any now is your chance. Let's say you now have an opportunity to harass Ashtar with all of the questions you have been wishing to know about! I will do my best to confuse you!

"Last tuesday, myself and several people in the East Bay were seeing an intense gold light grid being set up for the San Francisco Bay area, and what we believed to be Ashtar's ship working directly over the bay itself. Can you elaborate on what was transpiring?"

Caught in the act! There are many different activities that the light vehicles are attending to. One of them is assisting the lightworkers in stabilizing areas of the Earth's crust. We cannot do this of our own accord, but where there are lightworkers doing planetary healing, we take this as an invitation, and within the prime directive we are allowed to assist. Our mission is multidimensional, and sometimes we will be doing two or three, or two or three *hundred* things at once. So it is difficult to put it into one specific. We would also be working with the consciousness of those beings in that area, generally sub-consciously, but in your case you caught us in the act. It was not me individually, but it was one of the Command.

This is a good point to bring up here, that all of the work that we have been doing through this channel, to inform you, the informational aspect, is only about two or three percent of what we are actually doing. The bulk of the work is to empower each of you to be able to access Spirit and guidance directly, so that you are not dependent on others for your guidance. It is nice to share in this way, of course. While we are talking about light ships, we are clearing away your cobwebs, so you can get behind the controls yourselves. Have any of you noticed the presence of your Merkabah vehicles more intensely lately? When you call upon your light body in meditation, you are opening to the manifestation of your Merkabah. You might feel it surrounding you with an energy field that is very pleasant. You might hear a celestial tone, a signature of your individual Merkabah. We encourage you to connect with this. You can just say, "Please, Lord Sananda, help me to connect with my light body." Know that your Merkabah vehicle is always at hand and available to you.

"Ashtar, what's the difference between the Holy Spirit and my Higher Self?"

The Higher Self, in the context of these discourses, refers to your individual God-presence. The Holy Spirit is the feminine God-principle in action ... responsible for the birthing of universes, galaxies, and stars. So the Holy Spirit is, you could say, the feminine/receptive aspect, balancing the masculine/creative principle. It is the combination of these two energies which gives birth to the Son principle, the third aspect of the trinity. So you can ask for assistance from the Holy Spirit, from the Heavenly Father, or from the Son, represented in this universe by our Lord Sananda. Generally your prayers and requests will be directed to the proper source. It is your sincerity, your intention, the purity of your request, that decide, not whether you are doing it right or wrong: "Well, I'm not going to ascend. I have the wrong techniques!" It is not a matter specifically of language or techniques. You will use techniques, but techniques are only to enhance your direct experience of Spirit. Then you will become as Lord Sananda has said, as little children.

"I had an invisible visitor in March. He was asking for help and I couldn't understand what he was saying because he was talking in some kind of language. But

he was asking for help and I don't know what that was all about."

A rather disarming experience. There are many beings asking for assistance now, beings of fourth-dimensional manifestation, spirits without bodies. And there are also extraterrestrials hovering around planet Earth trying to learn the lesson of love, just as the beings of Earth are trying to learn it. So whatever they think they are here for, ultimately they are here to learn — in this laboratory — the lesson of love. Just send love and light to that being. You don't have to feel obligated to assist. Send them to me.

"Ashtar, it seems I have this overwhelming need for a sense of purpose. Yet the more I see the need, the more frustrated I get. Is it my impatience?"

Bingo! Sananda taught me that word. Always gets a laugh, he said. You have a purpose. Your purpose is unfolding. Give yourself to Spirit. Practice meditation. Don't be caught up in thinking that your Earth mission or your purpose has to be one particular external manifestation, one particular talent or skill or task. Your purpose is to learn what your purpose is, and surrender to it. It is a matter of surrender, not of intellectually creating it. You are fulfilling your purpose. Perhaps you are thinking you are not, but you are fulfilling it. It is just that at this stage there is still more veiling than you might wish for. And this goes for all of you. Though you might ask and pray for your veils to be removed, they can only be removed as you are prepared for that. Otherwise it would create disfunctionality in the systems, in the physical, emotional, and mental bodies. You would become discombobulated! I pulled that one out myself!

"Ashtar, can you speak to me about forgiveness and acceptance?"

As a being experiences divine love within their heart from Source, there arises a sense of love and forgiveness, of compassion. It is a spontaneous manifestation. It is not something you can create. It is something you can pray for, definitely. Ask Mother Mary, ask Lord Sananda to grant you this, to open your heart in this way, and it will be done. It is not easy. It has not been easy for beings living in a third-dimensional, dysfunctional world to always maintain this, but you will grow into it. I would suggest to start by loving yourself, regardless of what your judgments may be about your inadequacies. If you can forgive yourself, you will find it much easier to forgive others. You need a lot of grace to do this. So meditate, go within and ask for the grace to experience this. Ask and you shall receive. And then surrender, and just allow the unfoldment. You don't want to fight the flow, you want to go with the flow. You want to drift with the stream. You don't want to be paddling against the current. The universe, your Higher Self, are in control. They are directing you. They are carrying you along through every experience. Surrender is simply the ultimate acknowledgment that this is so. And then flow with the stream. Enjoy the scenery. Witness what you are here to witness and you will learn what you are here to learn. Each of you as a unique entity have specific programming, specific patterns to break, to transmute. You are doing this so that others who have these same patterns can overcome these patterns more easily. You are like the icebreakers in Antarctica. You have heavy hulls. You can crack the ice so that the weaker vessels can follow you. In giving yourself to Spirit, you create a very powerful hull so you will not be adversely affected as you crash through limitation.

"Ashtar, someone asked me what a lightworker was today. Would you give me your version of a lightworker?"

I'll let you give them your version! Because we are so close, I can tease you in this way. But there is always a kernel of truth. Anyone who gives themself consciously to following Spirit is a lightworker — anyone who loves the light and chooses the light, regardless of their source, regardless of what dimension they feel they might have come from, regardless of whether they feel they are a Starseed or a poor miserable earthling! Once you learn to love the light, you've got it. So don't worry about the rest.

So, before I say good night, I would just like to share a few more moments of meditation with you. I thank you for your involvement this evening, for your enjoyable questions. These interactions are very enjoyable to all of us, for we are a family of light. You are a family of lightworkers on a specific mission to this planet, and to the souls of this world. This is your overriding purpose, your overriding mission and destiny.

So just breathe with me for a few moments. I would like to call forth the energies of the light vehicles that are above us to surround and penetrate every cell of our bodies, penetrating the Earth, bringing healing energy into the Earth. Just breathe, and meditate on the light for a few moments. Allow this channel to open and assist you and heal you.

Hello, dear ones. This is Sananda with you. While you are basking in the beautiful emanations, I come briefly to share the energy of my love with you — to add it to the mix, to enhance the compassion within your hearts and the motivation to complete your Earth missions. I wish you each to know that I am with you always. The Hierarchy watches over you in each moment, waking or sleeping, always ready to assist. It is your responsibility to ask for the assistance you wish, and then to open to receive and allow. That is all that is required of you.

I wish to encourage you to practice accessing your individual God-presence, for this is the channel through which we can communicate and share our love directly, in ways that you can feel, see, and hear. There is far more love being administered than you are currently feeling or sensing. Take time in stillness to be with your spirit. Take time to retreat from external cares and give yourself to the ocean within. Allow a balance between the internal world and the external, so that you can be complete, so you can make your ascension with joy in your hearts, as my children.

We are real. The Ashtar Command is real. The light vehicles are here. The Great White Brotherhood is here, the angels. The universe opens its heart to planet Earth now. The love flows through the many messengers and is focused in you. It is yours to share. It is yours to radiate. It is yours to heal and to be healed. Call for assistance. We are yours to command. Enjoy your journey. And don't forget to have a sense of humor. You need it! I am always at your side like a trusty sword, to cut through confusion, to cut through miseries and sorrow. Love yourselves as best you can. It helps me in my work to love you.

On behalf of Ashtar, and all of the Masters who have assisted this evening, we send our love and blessings. We pledge our continuing support to all lightworkers all over the world. All who are sincere and pure of heart will benefit from this ascension experience. Goodnight.

CHAPTER NINE

THE LANGUAGE OF THE HEART

❧ Sananda ❧

Good evening. This is Sananda here with you this evening. Just relax yourselves and breathe, and allow my energies to enter your beings. I have a wonderful transmission this evening for you. As you are aware, it is a very special time, not only this time of year, the Easter season, but this time of man on planet Earth. Each of you have been working throughout this lifetime, and over many other lifetimes, to prepare yourselves for a quantum leap in experience, and to prepare this world to make that leap also. And now we stand on the cusp of this wonderful transformation. You are the forerunners. You have been feeling this transformation for some time, in your consciousness, and in your physical bodies. You have seen it at work in the world at large. It is going to be a wonderful experience. In fact, you could say it has already happened, as we watch from our perspective, and you from yours, this transformation filtering at last down into the physical. It is my wish for each of you, dear ones, that you will enjoy the blessings that are flowing at this time, that you will take full advantage of this opportunity. I would like to, with the assistance of each of you, offer to take these gatherings to a new level, to work with you at an even higher frequency, to bring through finer and subtler energies. I cannot do this alone. It is up to you to assist. But that is available to you now, to actually go beyond language and ideas into that wonderful realm of experience that proves those ideas and predictions about this planetary ascension are true.

You live in an incredibly divine and remarkable universe. The veils between what you have come to accept as reality, and what is now available to you, are becoming thinner and thinner. It is just a subtle surface tension in the collective consciousness that keeps the limited reality perspectives of Earth in place. Have you ever seen those little spider-like creatures that skim along the surface of lakes and streams? To them the surface of that water is as solid as ice. They simply skim across it on the surface tension that exists. And most human beings also are skimming on the surface tension of this illusory reality structure that you have agreed to create together. Though you are ones who would like to dive deeper, I think, or you would not be here.

There is a subtle programming that exists in human consciousness in this world. You could say it's an agreement. You could say it's a mass hypnosis. There is, in the minds of human beings, a connection with the collective consciousness, a part of which involves this agreement. You are born into this world in an open state, in an open consciousness. But immediately there begins a subtle programming. You are hypnotized to experience the world just as all other beings are experiencing it. You are hypnotized with incantations: "See the ball. This is a tree. Look at the nice kitty." And it proceeds from these simpler levels all the way through your more advanced training. And inherent within these dialogues, these incantations, you experience a subtler energy, a pattern of belief, a pattern of agreement. "Well, we have all agreed that trees look like this and feel like this, and because we all hold this same agreement, you will also." Most of you have not even seen the true presence of a tree. You have seen what you were programmed to see in that tree. Most of you have not seen human beings as the incredible luminous light beings that you are. Because within this agreement is also the chosen picture, the expression that you will accept of what a human being looks like.

To an enlightened being, to a God-conscious being, human beings are quite a bit more outrageous than simply a physical form. We witness you as incredible emanating energy fields, each of you very unique, anchored somehow into the third dimension by a physical structure, and yet not limited to that at all. What you are working to accomplish in meditation and spiritual practice is to disconnect that internal programming, to have a direct experience of reality with all of its marvels and wonders. The filters that hold you in limitation exist in the mind, in the ego perception. They are planted there via these hypnotic incantations. And the only way to transcend them completely is to reach the still point within you at the center of your being, to transcend that internal program, that ego you have come to accept as yourself. In those moments, within that stillness, your spirit and the magnificence of who you are can penetrate and reveal to you the visions of your higher aspects.

The surface tension that holds the reality programs of limitation in place is very strong on planet Earth. You could say there is a tendency for humanity to be quite entrapped in that, to the point of viewing beings who have another experience as being strange or weird or somehow dangerous. Many beings who have come here with a more evolved reality picture have been persecuted just because they were different. But at this time there are so many of you here. There is so much grace available. I and the many Masters are working to help you to create alternate reality patterns by helping you to reach that still point of divinity within you. For transcending the mind and all of its creations empowers you to see what truly exists. And what you will see is the inner light. What is it? It's you! You could say, "I am seeing God," but it's also you. That light is present in each moment, in every atom. Every being is radiating that light, and from that vantage point the world becomes a rather outrageous proposition. You see, it feels safe to live in limitation, to cling to the old patterns, the old programs. It takes courage, curiosity, surrender, and trust — and a great deal of self-love — to open to accept that which is being offered constantly to you by your own spirit.

The language of the collective consciousness of man is useful in performing your physical functions in this world, but it is very detrimental to your planetary and personal ascension. In fact, you could say it is coming apart a little at the edges, for the heavens are opening, and divine beings are falling out all over the place! I think some of you might have fallen from quite a height to be here. In fact, you might say that there was a tear in the fabric of heaven, and a lot of angels fell out and landed on this crazy world, with purpose — perhaps not remembering that purpose always, but knowing it in your hearts.

I am so overjoyed dear ones, to be with you this evening, to share this divine moment with you, and to see that you have selected to spend your time here with all of the choices that are available to you. It gives me great joy. I thank you. You see, I have the antidote. I am using it on you right now. The antidote is the language of the heart that I am speaking to you energetically, that I am focusing through you as I share this discourse. For the language of the heart, the language of light, is not spoken with words. It is transmitted on a ray of love, on a ray of energy — a subtle vibratory frequency. It is transformative. This energy is being broadcast to an entire planet, to all of the beings on this planet. And we watch as one by one you awaken, as that language of love, the language of the heart, de-programs your previous hypnotic state.

What happens? We could call it an awakening. It's just like being in a dream, you know? A dream that seems so real. When you are asleep, you are totally unaware that you are dreaming, that you are lying in a bed somewhere. In that moment, you are dreaming, and that is all there is. And you just have to do your best in that dream, whatever is going on, whether it's a beautiful experience or a nightmare, whatever is happening. But then, gradually or suddenly, there is an awakening. For a brief moment you realize, "Oh, this is a dream; now I'm going to wake up; now I am awake; now I have forgotten the dream." And this can all happen in two or three seconds. So just as you experience that awakening, you are also experiencing an awakening from the programmed collective consciousness of Earth. And you have all experienced these moments of clarity, moments of wisdom, moments of pure and utter faith and knowingness — these awakenings. You're having one right now. I'm doing my best to share it with you.

In India, they say that "truth is the consciousness of bliss." Well, truth is truth, but it is quite true that when you experience it you become very blissful. So open yourself to that bliss that is constantly flowing. It is not only flowing when you are in a spiritual gathering; it is always there. It is life, the life force. If you are breathing, it is there. If you're not experiencing it, you are identifying with a lesser reality, with another pattern.

It requires, on your part, patience and persistence. For though you may have moments of sudden illumination, where you know what I am speaking of is true, it takes a consistent effort, a consistent spiritual practice, to learn to live in that state beyond fear, beyond limitation, connected to the higher-dimensional aspects of yourself. We are here always, encouraging you to go within in meditation, to breathe. Let the breath still the mind, stop the internal dialogue, open your being to receive. It's the inner door, you know? If you will take time each day to meditate, to go within, to look at the inner light, to meditate on the breath, you will find your connection with the unspeakable presence of God. If you will take time to practice, you will learn to live in that peaceful place.

Self-mastery, as we have mentioned many times, is required: to master your creations, the creations of the mind. Haven't you noticed that your projections are coming to fruition much more rapidly? That only means you are learning your lessons more and more quickly. Offer your experiences up to Spirit in each moment. Don't be tricked by the internal dialogue that tries to keep you in a limited state, but offer that up to Spirit as well. Affirm. Pray. Pull out all of the stops, whatever you can do. Whatever works for you, use that, and ask to be guided always to the next step, to the next deeper level.

Last time we spoke of union, of God-realization, and that is the experience you will have. You will attain it through your own mastery, and by grace. Don't forget the grace! You can spend a lot of time trying to do it yourself, or you can call for assistance.

So my friends, I would like to say again that I am most grateful that you have chosen to be with me this evening. It is a very special time, and a very special time for this world. For the energies are shifting, and will shift very radically from this point onward. You will need to apply yourselves to your spiritual practices if you wish to ride these waves and have the most direct and enjoyable journey into that infinite state. You will be challenged, but you will be extremely well-rewarded for every effort that you make.

There are many who feel that they cannot meditate, that it is too difficult, that their minds are too active. So start by praying. And ask for assistance. Do affirmations.

And then don't meditate, just breathe. Wherever you are in that moment, just take a breath. Focus your attention one hundred percent on just that breath, and then on just the next one. It only takes a split second of stillness to feel the grace, to feel that transformation. For those who have the ability to connect with Spirit, these days to come will be filled with marvels, wonders, and bliss — and also with challenges. But the challenges will be welcomed as opportunities for growth. For those who have only the desire to escape reality, to dive into the dream state, to cover their heads as the sun rises, there will be more difficulties. I call on each of you to accept my offer and my challenge: to be with me now, to open your heart and allow these energies of love into your lives. And don't forget, my friends, to have a sense of humor about it. In fact, at times the only thing that you will have to cling to may be your sense of humor, as you experience strange manifestations and purifications within your personalities. Sometimes you just have to laugh at yourself, knowing that it's not real. It's totally amazing, truly, how you could get so much divinity and energy into such small packages, and even more how you try with all of your might to cling to such limited perspectives while the universe attempts to pour forth incredible energies of expansion. Really, it is very humorous!

I am asking each of you, in my own way, to open to the language of the heart, the language of love, the language of light in your lives. It is more important than all of your ideas put together. Your ideas, whether they are right or wrong, or partially right, will all have to be surrendered in that moment of ascension. You can't carry them through the gate: it is too narrow. You have to let go of your baggage. There is only room for the true Self, which is always humble, and yet powerful. So accept the opportunity that is before you to receive these new frequencies, these subtler, finer, and yet more powerful energies. Let them flow through and transform you. Go into the still space within, and allow. If you want to spend most of your day being crazy, that's fine. In fact, you probably will. But please spend at least a portion of your day with Spirit. And then that portion will grow, expand, and the other will diminish. Sorrow will be transmuted and dissolved.

It's really very simple. In fact, it becomes more and more simple as it goes along. We began our teachings through this channel with some very amazing predictions and ideas. These have been recorded, and you can read them or listen to them. Now we are going into finer realms. I am opening the doorways that you will walk through, into realms that cannot be described or explained except with the language of the heart.

So, at this point it is customary for me to ask what I can do to serve you. Have you questions or areas you wish me to address? You may ask if you have any questions.

"Could you tell us a little bit about the nature of the photon belt?"

It represents a physical, scientific manifestation, at a rather more gross level, of the transformation that is taking place. As the Earth moves into this realm of higher consciousness, it is also moving into a new realm of space, you could say. There are many ideas and predictions; most of them are a little overblown from my perspective, as though you were awaiting something physical to come and conk you on the head and suddenly transform you. It is this new space, you could say, that is marking the end of the old planetary cycle, causing the transformation of the Earth to take place on a physical level. It is a part of that. Also, it is just another manifestation of Spirit. You will know what it is by experiencing it, just as you know everything else. You know who I am by experiencing me in your being, and you will experience the photon belt in this way as well. It is all part of the divine drama that is unfolding, nothing to be overly worried about. In fact, you could say it is another expression of grace.

"I've been receiving a lot of electrical shocks recently. I was wondering if that was part of the changes in our bodies that we're going through?"

It is part of the awesome transformation of consciousness within your physical body — provided you have not stuck your hand in an outlet! The transformation is radical, and you will all experience it in your own unique ways. As you give yourself to Spirit, the body comes along in its own way, and it experiences many strange phenomena. For some it is more graceful. For some it is shocking. Most likely it's just a wake-up call, some shock therapy from your spirit. It is a temporary phenomenon; I can tell you that.

"I've been receiving lots of information recently from various sources describing the fact that in the future we might need to put our energy into dome housing or underground housing. Could you comment on that, please?"

There will definitely be transformations of the planet — climatic and Earth changes, as you know. The degree that this will be necessary is still dependent upon the consciousness of man, and upon nothing else. At this point you could say, based on the consciousness of man, you are in for a rather rough ride. And if indeed this is the case, and your spirit is guiding you, then by all means follow that guidance. This does not mean that everyone needs to head for the hills or live in caves. It is a matter of your spirit guiding you to what is best for you. Whether you will be in physical form at the time of these radical changes depends upon your own destiny path and your own choice regarding physical ascension. We have guided human beings to choose the ascension path, to practice this, and to allow for the possibility and probability that you will have the chance to be lifted via the ascension or by evacuation, if necessary. In either case, you will not need a dome or a cave. There are many who probably will not take advantage of this opportunity. They will have to perhaps experience that which has been referred to as the tribulation, or you could say, more intense wake-up calls. For them, following spirit in this way could be a very wise course of action. So I can only say for you individually, as for all individuals, that your spirit will guide you to the areas of the planet, to the realms of consciousness, and to the activities that you will need to perform, in order to experience this transformation as gracefully as possible.

There is another point I would like to make. Each experience you have, in fact, is created by you, by the projections you make based upon your experience of reality. I have been encouraging you this evening to go to a deeper level, to recognize your divinity, and to prepare for the ascension experience. From that vantage point you will have an entirely different experience of planetary transformation than one who is in limited consciousness. In fact, every being exists within their own unique reality, especially once you have broken through the mass hypnosis we have been speaking of this evening. You will find that this is true. So you can choose how you want to experience the planetary transformation. We have recommended choosing the spiritualization of matter, the ascension path, and to do so slightly ahead of the planet herself. For the planet herself must make that transformation. The Earth may be transformed in such a way that it will not be recognizable, or there will be very little recognizable from what you are perceiving now. If you look at this transformation only from a physical perspective, you could feel fearful about it, you could feel that you are in an unsafe environment. But your spiritual practice will teach you that you are always safe, that you are always protected. And indeed, you can live in a state where there will be no need for you to be harmed, even though you might exist in the middle of one of the Earth changes. For each being in the midst of an apparent cataclysm also creates the reality that they experience, the level of intensity they need for their own awakening. If you can grasp this concept you can exist in freedom on this planet, even in the midst of external chaos, for the chaos will not penetrate your consciousness. It will be a dream compared to the reality that you are experiencing, the harmony.

So again, it is your choice. First of all, give yourself to spiritual practice. Let this be your foundation. In doing so you will become more and more clear. You will be guided. And if you feel inspired to build a dome, to move to a new location, to change your livelihood, whatever, by all means give yourself to that. It is a unique path for each of you.

"Can you tell us a little about the return of the Spiritual Hierarchy? We have been told that before we actually enter into the photon belt that there would be a return and a mass landing. Also could you tell us about the return of the Christ, and will we see him as an apparition within this time?"

It is your choice as to how you wish to experience these things. How you experience the Christ is dependent upon your level of consciousness, for the Christ is with you now in this moment. If you could raise the frequency of your vision, you would see me standing behind this body, holding it within my energy field, and that would be for you an apparition of the Christ. There is a very good possibility of mass landings. There is a very good possibility of mass evacuations. In part, the return of the Spiritual Hierarchy is you, only you haven't fully awakened to that possibility yet. And it is also me. Here I am! I can't say much for the package, but the connection is clear. This contact is another way to experience the Hierarchy. And there will be more marvels, more wonders yet to come. As humans elevate their consciousness and their ability to perceive the Ascended Masters, the Masters can lower their vibratory rates and meet you in the middle, so that you can interact with us in a more direct way. Perhaps we will go beyond this channeling experience altogether. This is only a temporary phenomenon, you know.

Let's create a new soft drink, something like "Photon Brew." It would have to be very sparkly and bubbly, and you could say, "Oh, those are the photons. As the photons explode on your taste buds, feel your consciousness rise!" I am also available for new age marketing consultations; I know what you want to hear. Most of the time I will not say that. You want to hear that you will enter the photon belt, and suddenly you will be walking down the street and you will be enlightened — through no efforts of your own, but simply because a photon struck you on the head — whatever a photon is.

You know it's funny. We say these words and we don't even know if we're all thinking the same thing, especially those great New Age terms like "photon belt," and even more simple terms like "tree." Everyone thinks that when another person sees a tree they are both seeing exactly the same thing. It is part of the hypnosis. And when we say love, you have reference points called memories within you to draw upon, and you also have the experience of the moment, yet each of you have a unique experience of love. This is why we must resort to the language of the heart, rather than the language of the mind, to get our message across in ways that cannot be filtered or altered. We have tried our best to bring through spoken messages in these channelings, and we have been always surprised at the diversity of the reactions to the very same channelings. Two people will hear the same discourse, the same sentence, and have completely unique reactions. Oftentimes it is completely opposite. That is one reason it is necessary to have a sense of humor. You see, this body is just blowing air at you — through this mouth, this throat, this tongue, these teeth — and you think that there is a meaning in these syllables simply because you have heard them many times before. Unfortunately, this is still necessary. But know that along with these syllables and vowels and sound patterns there is also a transformational energy: the language of the heart. If someone is speaking a spiritual discourse, and you are not hearing the language of the heart, you'd better run. For it is just another subtle form of hypnosis, another way of programming you to believe a certain way. That is not teaching. A teacher imparts an experience directly. And though we are limited somewhat by this physical form, and by the consciousness that rides around in it, you can feel the transformational energy that comes along with these words. What we are trying to do is to help each of you to experience directly the Christ energy, the energy that you are.

"I've been blessed with many people coming into my life, and I sense that there is a soul coming into my life and that our energies will assist us in going forward on our journey. Can you say something about this?"

Someone besides me? Yes, but for you, even as this manifests, you will have to surrender and detach from your projection. I would suggest you offer it up to Spirit and say, "When it is highest wisdom for this particular person to re-enter my life, let me recognize that person, and let me enjoy that interaction and maximize the learning that is there," without projecting a lot of expectations.

"Lord Sananda, I want to know what we do when we're in that transitional stage?"

Pray like hell! I wouldn't trade with you, put it that way. Why do you think we're not manifesting in physical bodies? From this safe vantage point I can easily tell you that all is well. You see, there are many strategies you can use. It depends on what works for you. When meditation is difficult, pray and ask for assistance. Offer up your experiences, offer up your pain, your frustration, whatever you have. Affirm that you are one with Spirit. Practice the I AM affirmations. And in those moments, just breathe. Stopping the internal dialogue is the key to entering into that state of grace. We can come through and force it, jam it, as we do sometimes. There are beings who have taken many drugs and other herbal formulas to try and jam that dialogue, and they have experienced other realms, other realities. But the key is to be able to do it consciously, and to maintain it gracefully. It takes patience. It takes persistence. I cannot remove your lessons. For those intensities that you experience are something that you have programmed yourself to experience, that your Higher Self has attracted to teach you: to teach you the nature of attachment, to guide you gently or perhaps more forcefully into a state of surrender. So you attract the teachings and the intensity of the teachings that you require. If, on one hand, you are praying for divine intervention, to experience God-consciousness and ascension, while on the other hand continuing to create negative patterns, something has got to give. And as your consciousness is becoming more and more subtle, more and more sensitive, those limited experiences, challenges, frustrations seem to be ever more difficult, ever more painful. It is part of being in a physical body. There will always be challenge when one is inhabiting a physical form. The physical form, as beautiful a creation as it is, is still bound to physical laws.

"How can we assist on this plane in exposing all truths?"

Well, I would suggest that you simply expose the truth in your own being and leave the rest to me. The truth is something that you become, and in becoming it, it radiates. It is not an idea that you expose to the public consciousness. Exposing the ideas of spirituality to the mass consciousness only creates a subtler level of programming. It only creates another reality picture. And that reality picture does not express truth more than any other. You must use the language of the heart, the language that radiates through your own channel, from your own personal experience, and this will expose and release the attachment to the mass consciousness. What I am asking each of you to do, is to open to the possibility that everything you know is wrong! In other words, all ideas are equally ludicrous. So to expose the world to what you may feel is an important truth is just exposing the world to your reality pictures. To expose the Earth and the mass consciousness to truth itself, you must become it: you must be the light. And then when they look in your eyes they will receive a transmission of that language of love and light that cannot be spoken. As far as the illusion being stripped away, we are taking care of that.

So, perhaps we could conclude this evening with a little meditation. If you keep coming to these gatherings, you are going to get tired of hearing that word. But if you keep coming to these gatherings, you will soon go into a higher state of awareness, and you will no longer care what words I'm saying. You will only have the ears to hear the language of the heart. So relax and breathe. Feel my energies penetrating your being, entering your space. I am working with the heart energy, opening your beings, balancing your chakras, transforming your energy fields. You have only to breathe, or look at the light, or listen to the inner music — whatever way Spirit presents itself to you. Just know that you are surrounded by a beautiful energy field within and without, and relax your body, all of your muscles. Relax your mind. Give yourself entirely to the breath. Let that be your exclusive focus for just a few moments.

So my friends, I would like to conclude this evening by thanking you once again for your attendance. I have truly enjoyed sitting with you. I would like to say, again, how important this lifetime is, how blessed you are to be inhabiting human bodies at this particular juncture of human history — how blessed you are to be on the spiritual path, to be preparing for the ascension experience. There are many beings who would give anything to be in your shoes, many etheric beings. The transformations and challenges that you face will be transmuted quickly. More and more joy, more and more light and love will be yours. Accept every experience with equanimity and surrender. And trust, always trust. No matter what experience comes your way, it is highest wisdom for you in that moment. Don't try to escape from earthly reality in the spiritual experience. Bring the spiritual experience to bear. Surround your earthly life with that grace. Take advantage of the opportunities that are available to you now. The advantage of having a physical body now is immense. It is the ideal platform for ascension. It is an ideal platform from which to experience the multidimensional manifestations of God. So enjoy that. And always ask for assistance.

I am with each of you. And I pledge that I will always be with you, surrounding you with love, light, and grace. You are precious to me. The humblest, most sincere beings are most precious to me. Those who can access their child-like nature, their innocence, are ones that I can identify and play with. Those who are sophisticated and serious and intense are less accessible to me, though they are also in my heart. So I look forward to being with you, dear ones, in many ways. Enjoy this holy season of Earth. And remember to attune yourself to the language of the heart. For this is where you will learn all that you need to know: that which cannot be spoken, but which can be known. So, I love you all so much. Good night.

CHAPTER TEN

LETTING GO

❧ St. Germain ❧

Good evening. Nice to be here with you this evening. This is St. Germain. I come to you this evening with a great deal of love and light, with healing energies for you who have been serving here on planet Earth, who have been working to open yourselves to receive the next level, the next initiation. So whatever the next step is for you individually, that is what I will be working on this evening. As a group we will be doing some healing work. Perhaps we will have a little picnic. I ask that you relax yourselves and breathe as you sit with me. We will boost the energies so that you will be more comfortable in your skins this evening. Lately it has been a little bit difficult perhaps to be here. I notice many of you wanting to make an early getaway! But you must take care which exit you choose. Choose a higher-dimensional exit. So we will be working to smooth out your energies a bit after these transformational weeks that you have been experiencing.

In the overall scheme of life, I have noticed that the energies and manifestations within any given dimension, or octave, of existence are created largely by the thoughtforms and beliefs of the beings who exist in that dimensional octave. And there is a tendency for human beings to view external situations and sociological conditions as static, to feel that you have just dropped into this strange place where all of this was going on and will be going on after you. I would like to share another perspective: that in each moment of existence, that which is created is created spontaneously out of the thoughtforms and belief projections of the beings in existence. That is, the beings of planet Earth are holding the patterns in their consciousness, in their beliefs and thoughtforms, that are perpetuating the experiences that they are having here. All of the situations that you perceive are spontaneous creations. So in seeking to heal the Earth and her inhabitants in preparation for a higher-dimensional experience, it serves you to change, and to assist others to change their beliefs, their thoughtforms, their projections. You are all focusing Spirit through yourselves in this creative process you call life.

You who have given yourselves to the spiritual path, if you have not dedicated yourselves one hundred percent, I invite you now to do so. The most important work that you can do is to transform yourselves by transforming your thoughts, beliefs, and projections about the very nature of your reality, about the nature of life, about what it means to be alive here as a physical being. You know, there are physical beings walking around on Earth in the state of bliss. There are many more walking around in states of alienation, anger, or fear. It is necessary that we work together to transform those negative patterns into patterns that are reflective of the divine plan.

There is nothing inherently wrong with physical world existence. In fact, it is a very beautiful manifestation of God's grace. Each moment is a blessing unfolding, a spontaneous creation. Because the energies of grace and light were misqualified at some point in time, and continue to be, you find this world experiencing lesser states. By changing yourselves, by allowing higher-dimensional energies to enter your beings to give you new models of perception, new beliefs and possibilities, you will be transformed into those who can create manifestations that are in alignment with the divine plan. You could say it was in the divine plan for density to exist, for so-called negative emotions and experiences to manifest as a learning for beings in this realm. You can also say that this is not meant to be a permanent condition. You stand on the cusp of this new age, in which all of this will be transformed. In fact, you are the agents. You are the secret agents. Each of you have your own secret code, "007" or whatever. It is your responsibility to awaken to this secret code, this secret combination within you that is the unique path for you as individuals to experience self-realization, so that you might act as agents of change to transform those negative patterns.

If you have not experienced the light, how can you be a lightworker? You can aspire to it. You can attempt to live in alignment with certain rules and practices. But truly, it is time to awaken to the light itself. That is essential. That is your food. To become a lightworker you must change. You are changing. You have been transforming. This work that we do together is quite transformative. For in our gatherings we create an interdimensional doorway through which my energies, and the energies of many Masters, can flow through your being and give you new and subtle energetic models. And before you know it, you find you are patterning yourself after a higher-dimensional manifestation of existence. Before you know it, you find that your old ways of being and thinking seem heavy, seem difficult to maintain. It seems more work than it is worth to become angry and to stay that way, or to feel jealousy and to hold it in your body as if it were real. And all of these energies that you transmute by experience are being lifted up, transmuted. What remains of you is your divine Higher Self, still in the physical body of course, but experiencing the bliss, experiencing the real. This is the entire purpose of our gatherings, to help you to experience this. Once you experience it, there is no longer a need for external teachings, for external models. For the model that is most suitable for you is already existing within you. It is up to you to find your secret agent number. What is the pure reflection of yourself, with all of your divine gifts and talents and skills? What is it that you came here to manifest? In order to find out, you have to open yourself and surrender to the path of transmuting these old patterns. Just allow them to be lifted. We will do some work later on this to assist you, some violet flame work.

We encourage you to come more fully into this moment, for this moment is all that truly exists. It is a spontaneous creation. It is being created in each moment. It is not a static situation that you can take for granted. And in that moment is where you find your hidden code, your Higher Self, your God-presence awaiting you. It is something to let go to. It is something to simply allow. It is not something you construct with your mind or your ideas. It is already perfect within you, who you are and what you are here to do, perfectly manifested! A divine jewel; this is how I perceive you. Perhaps you have a little shadow around the edges. That's all it is, you know: a thin veil remaining, a subtle belief in limitation, an identification with the ego-self. The divine Higher Self enters and swallows up the ego, and you find that you are a being of love and delight, and there is nothing that you need to change because you are a perfect reflection. It is something to surrender to, something to let go to.

We have spoken many times in our discourses, myself and the many Masters, about the experience of surrender. This is key for you. I would like to discuss this briefly. I'd like to put my two cents worth in. The idea of surrender can be very complicated. You find yourself wondering, "Well, what shall I do this day? I want to surrender my life to Spirit." Well, what does that mean? What action does that entail? What action does that eliminate? From my experience, surrender is simply being in the moment, opening your eyes and looking at what's in front of you, and doing that. What is the universe presenting you with? Maybe your idea is that you wish to surrender to God by sitting in meditation all day long until you achieve self-realization. And yet, when you open your eyes, you find there is no food in your refrigerator. The lights have been turned off, the phone line is dead, and there is a large truck at your door. Perhaps the sheriff is there as well, with his slip of paper. Well, you surrendered yourself out of a place to live. You surrendered yourself to the street (!), when perhaps I might suggest, surrender for you would have been to recognize your situation and get a job, to find some way to earn that which you need to maintain your life, so that you have a home, and food to eat, and a place to meditate.

Your Higher Self is attracting to you all the experiences that you are receiving, as a teaching. If you just open to that, you will find more and more that you are recognizing God's play behind all of these experiences. Recognizing that "All right, I can surrender to this. In this moment this is my path. I don't have to worry about whether or not I am going to attain realization this day or tomorrow or the next day. I have only to be in this moment." And if you can break into that moment, that spontaneity of existence, you will find that this is where the joy dwells. The joy is there waiting for you. That which you thought you would achieve through some spiritual practice was already there. You just let go. You just surrender to it. That is your path, you see. It is unique for each of you individually. Whatever is before you. If things come up before you and your heart tells you that is not your way, then that is your path, a lesson in discernment. It is one choice after another, isn't it? Sometimes you just want to be left alone: "I can't decide anything else. Just leave me alone. I don't know." Sometimes you just have to be irresponsible for a while and surrender to that. Surrender to the playfulness of existence. In your awakening to each moment, you will come in contact with the people, and events, and experiences that are your path, that are your signposts. You never know the magnificence of your path until you begin to truly let go to it and live it in each moment.

Offer every experience up to Spirit. Offer it up through the channel of your Higher Self, back to the Source. Maybe you don't know what it is. Maybe you don't know what it means. Maybe all you need to know is that it is another thing to offer up. Each moment, offer it up. Offer it up on your breath. Your breath is a tool to bring you back into the moment and back into contact with your spirit. It is perfectly adapted to that. Your breath is like a door that takes you to a space that is deeper than mind, deeper than intellect or emotion, to a quiet place inside of you. *That* is the inter-dimensional doorway that you will walk through. That is your inner door.

To recognize your blessings is a grace: to recognize what you have been given, what the universe is offering you. In that recognition your life takes on a new meaning. It takes on a purpose. It becomes filled with love and bliss. You realize that you have a ringside seat to an incredible event, an incredible transformation. You are experiencing it and you are helping to facilitate it. As you are beings of the third-dimensional reality of the Earth plane, your thoughtforms, your awareness, alter the awareness and thoughtforms of the collective consciousness. And it does not take half the population of the Earth in order for this new consciousness to arise. You are going to witness many wonders. From what I have been able to glimpse, you are going to witness transformations that you cannot even imagine. I cannot tell you how each of you will experience them, for that is your unique path. I can only say that you will. There is so much joy, so much happiness awaiting you. It is already existing, here in this moment, for you to open to. And yet, to whatever degree you are experiencing it in this moment, there is so much more. Every breath is an opportunity to let more in. In your lives, whatever you are doing, whatever you are working at, you are breathing. There is the breath, and you can use that breath to open and receive more grace.

If there is one thing I have learned in working with human beings, it is patience. Once you have experienced self-realization and the ascension, it seems so very simple. It seems that you should just be able to say the word, speak about it for a few moments, and everyone would suddenly attain it. It seems *that* near at hand, that easy. And yet the path winds through many experiences that you have given yourself to learn from, and there patience is required. You must start with where you are now. Surrender to that, accept that, love that. Love the person that you are right now, for by loving you are healed. Just as we love you unconditionally, you can begin to love yourselves and others unconditionally. And that holds the space for transformation. It holds the space that allows a human being to feel that it is safe to change, that it is safe to open to something other than the mundane consciousness. It has to feel safe. That is one reason why we have these gatherings. We create a place where it is safe for you to simply be who you are, where the boss isn't going to walk in and say, "What about those papers? They were supposed to be on my desk yesterday!"

Because the universe is benevolent and compassionate, and the Creator's energies are unconditionally loving, there is always an open door for you as human beings. The Creator witnesses you and waits, and like your Father will say, "Well, have you had enough? Have you experienced enough of separateness? Very good, you have experienced that. I have something else for you. When you are ready, it is here. If you are not ready yet, I will just create another world where you can go and experience more limitation until you are ready." Total compassion. Total unconditional love and acceptance.

We who have experienced what you will experience have slightly less patience, in that we are telling you to "Get on with it!" Why wait? You are going to have to go through those doorways, those transformations, those processes of change, no matter what. It is not a matter of simply waiting it out. "Oh, I'll just wait until the new age manifests and then I'll be there." You have to go through the process. You have to go through the release, through the clearing, through the healing, whether it is challenging or simple in any moment. And no matter whether it is challenging or simple, blissful or difficult, that is your path and you are on it. Just be that in that moment. Feel what you are feeling. Pray. Ask to be taken into the next level of consciousness, the next step for you. Ultimately you will experience self-realization, where there will be union and bliss, where there will be no more false identity of ego. So start where you are. Each day give yourself to spiritual practice. Whatever is working for you, continue that. Open to meditation. Open to the breath, to the inner light. Know that within you exists a window on infinity. As vast as your world is externally, it is far more vast internally. There are realms of consciousness and experience that you can access only by going within. This body is the vehicle. You see how blessed you are.

In between complaining about how difficult it is to be in a human body and wishing the world were not quite so evil, you could perhaps take some time each day to meditate upon this inner space. Recognize just how blessed you are to even have this vehicle, this vehicle that is your launching pad into the infinite. It is the foundation. It is a perfect manifestation, a perfect training device for beings who wish to experience the Creator at every dimension of existence.

The power of your affirmations and prayers now is many, many times what it was in the past. The power of your thoughts and projections to create is many, many more times more powerful. I have spoken many times of self-mastery, self-mastery as the purification of your energy projections. The purification of your manifestations comes about through the change which takes place within you, the change that you are now undergoing. The more pure you become, the more accelerated your path. Believe it or not, you are each experiencing the maximum growth that you can, the maximum grace, the maximum light. If you want more of it, you have only to ask. And then look out. Here it comes, sometimes more than you bargained for! "Oh, I didn't know it was going to mean this, the total surrender of my ego. I thought it was just going to be some beautiful experiences of love and light that I could write a book about." And perhaps you begin your book, and you find that the path takes you to total self-destruction! "Wait a minute, I'm still on the third chapter. What is this dissolution of my ego? What is this dissolution of all my desires to be a famous author?" All of that — all those desires, all of those ego-projections — are being transmuted. You are experiencing them to see what they bring you, and learning from that. But one way or the other, they are going. Because we need to have some beings on Earth willing to create the kingdom of heaven in their lives, to counteract the collective consciousness, to transform it. And it will; it will be transformed.

It's very simple. You change your thoughts, your projections, your beliefs through experiencing Spirit, and the world around you changes. And the beings that you encounter are affected also. Maybe all they can say is, "Hmm. I want some of that, whatever that is." They feel it, as a heart-to-heart communication. Open up. Open to transmit and receive. You are the channels. You are the inter-dimensional doorways walking around on foot. Be a little more outrageous in your expression of the Self. Try some new things. For some of you, a new thing would be to actually meditate! I have a list, you know. I won't name any names. It is not necessary to embarrass you. You know who you are. Look at it this way. If you have not yet begun to meditate, you can meditate for five minutes a day and it will be a great improvement. You will really feel something. If you're already meditating two, three, four hours per day, an extra five minutes won't make that much difference. The important thing is to give some of your quality time to your spirit.

So, I think we're ready for our picnic. I would like to share a little bit of guided meditation. That is what I intend by the word picnic. I would like to take you to my personal picnic ground, to share with you some healing energies, some transmutational energies. I will assist you in releasing those old patterns, thoughtforms, energies that you might find that you are ready to let go of. Don't worry — it won't hurt a bit.

Just relax yourselves. Take some deep breaths and allow your bodies to relax totally: your legs, your arms, your bellies, your necks, your jaw, your facial muscles. We are going to have a little bit of a barbecue here. We are going to barbecue your karma burgers. And I am going to gobble them up! Sorry, you don't get to eat any tonight. I feel ravenous!

Know that you are surrounded with love and light. There is a beautiful column of energy surrounding this room, containing us all this evening. Here we are surrounded by many Masters. I ask you to visualize, in the center of our circle, a narrow column of light coming from above. A violet ray of energy, coming from above, down through the center of our circle and into the Earth. It may look to you like a flaming energy, however you wish to visualize it. Just allow it to descend in the center of our circle. Now, in silence, I ask you to tune in to whatever it is within you that you wish to transmute, that you wish to have released. Whatever energies you feel, whatever veils you feel, now is your opportunity to offer them up. Stretch out your arms and place them in the violet flame column. And as you do so, the flames extend and widen, becoming more powerful. And the flames carry up any dense energies to the higher dimensions for transmutation. Let the violet flames in the column of the violet ray expand slowly through your bodies to surround this entire room.

Just take a few moments and relax and breathe and feel these energies, whatever they feel like to you, however you experience them. If you wish an intensification, ask for it. If you wish for it to diminish a bit, ask for that.

Now I ask you to just allow the violet flames to once again concentrate in the center of the circle, carrying with them all dense energies, leaving you feeling purified, clear and open. And then visualize the column rising back out of sight above you.

So, dear ones, thank you from the bottom of my being for coming to be with me this evening, for spending this time gathering together for your own benefit and for the benefit of this planet and all beings. I know that you are often unaware of the totality of the experience that you create in gathering together, the totality of the experience of healing that extends in all directions through this dimension. I can only thank you for doing so. It is vital at this time. Call upon me, whenever you wish to work with the violet flame energies, when you wish assistance in your meditation practice, or in letting go and surrendering in each moment. I will be with you. Good evening.

CHAPTER ELEVEN

⤞ Mother Mary & Sananda ⤝

Good evening, dear ones, this is Mother Mary here with you. I'm here to warm up the room energetically for the next speaker. I thank you for your love and support, and for your attendance this evening at this gathering. Together, we can accomplish great things. We will be working with you individually as we are also working with the group energy, using that group energy in a healing for the Earth. If you feel yourself being energized this evening, know that you are acting as an interdimensional doorway, or channel, for energies of healing to come through. And I ask you to allow this. Just relax yourselves and breathe.

At this time on planet Earth, and in each of your lives, you are experiencing many transformations, as you are well aware. These transformations, these energy infusions that you have experienced, and that you will continue to experience, have led you to go within, to go in search of a higher experience, a deeper connection with Source — both as a service to planet Earth and its inhabitants, and as a sanctuary for your own protection and security, for your own peace and harmony. Simply to exist in the physical world in a third-dimensional consciousness can no longer bring you the satisfaction it once may have, for all beings are being thrust into an experience of communion with the higher power that exists. You could say the Higher Self within you is being activated, is calling for your attention more and more strongly all the time.

You are being called upon to learn the cosmic laws that exist and to apply those laws in your lives, to humble yourselves a bit, to receive instruction from within and without concerning ways that you can realize your life's destiny, your individual missions here on this Earth at this time. And all the ways that any of you experience this energy of God, however you wish to label it, are perfectly sacred for you. Each individual on the spiritual path has unique characteristics and abilities, unique ways of perceiving the presence of the Creator. It is not so important, from my perspective, how you go about achieving this communion, this new consciousness. If you are open, you will be led. You will be guided to the path that is most direct and easiest for you. What I do recommend is that you follow that path.

Every soul is called, and every soul has the opportunity to respond. And in your response to that call, you affect other souls, you affect the planetary consciousness. And when there are enough souls in alignment and heeding that call, following that path actively, there will be major transformations in the planetary consciousness. So you see how important it is, my dear ones, that each of you be sincere and honest in your own hearts about what you are here to do, that you open to the love and compassion that are flowing through, altering your perspective, transforming you. It is important. You could say the time for dawdling is at an end. There is never enough time to realize your Creator, and there is always enough time. There is always just enough time for you to come into alignment and to make the connection.

That is the first step, just making the connection — recognizing and experiencing practically that which is divine within you, that which is within you that is one with the Source. You need to have a practical experience, a real experience. And once that connection is made — allowing those energies to flow through you consistently in your meditations, in your spiritual practice, in your prayers and affirmations, and honestly addressing the possibility that you can merge with that energy — then you will return home.

The longing that exists within you to return home is growing. As the energies of transformation pour through this dimension, all dimensions, a harmonic is created. You could say your soul is attuned to that vibration, and in its awakening, a longing for union, a longing for home fills your being. Perhaps the longing was always there subtly, but now it is growing. It is a longing that will not be satisfied by anything less than the realization of complete union with Source.

I wish to share with you my love and my support. And I am but one of many who are here to assist you. In contacting higher-dimensional teachers, you are taught to surrender your limited personalities. You give up your negative emotions, offering them up as the divine Self replaces them and fills the void, fills the vacuum within you. As you are still holding denser energies, it is necessary to continue this process of release, of opening, of offering up within you that which no longer serves you, to make room for your divine Higher Self.

This process is not difficult. It is most simple. In fact, it is so simple that most of you aren't getting it! We have witnessed you attempting to recreate perfection, when really you only have to let go and just fall into it. There are many who will tell you that the spiritual path is very difficult, that it requires great self-sacrifice and mighty acts of discipline. You can create it to be that way if you wish, but this is not necessary. In each moment you are alive you have access. You have the keyhole in your heart and you have the key in your hand. You have the divine holy breath that sustains you; that is your focus. When you are confused, just breathe. Come into contact with the breath and let it bring you into the presence of Spirit. It is so simple. It is never in the world; it is always within you. No matter what you may do in this world, the fundamental truth of your divine nature always remains. The doorway to that divine nature is always within you and can be accessed by stilling the mind through breathing, by meditation. In your prayers, in your affirmations, you seek to create a stillness in your being so that you can feel the subtler energies. The subtlest energy is the Source! And it is also the most powerful energy! You can learn to channel this energy in many ways. You can learn to surrender to this energy and let it flow through you in many beautiful ways. And it always feels like love.

So dear ones, don't be in fear; be in love. Love yourselves as we love you. Offer up your self-criticism, your self doubts, your ego-infatuation. They are all the same. They are all shadows across the face of the sun: all illusion, all separateness. Know that I love you, dear ones. I offer my services to each of you in many ways, but always my love and compassion assist you. So, please, call upon me in your moments of joy and in your moments of sorrow. All the moments that are part of this earthly life are divine … divine opportunities to go deeper. I thank you for your attention. Good day.

Greetings, my friends. It gives me great pleasure to be with you. I am Sananda. Our love for you is so overwhelming, at times it is difficult to speak. In the midst of this planet in transition, on a world of fear, anger, and violence, you have chosen to take another course. You have chosen wisely to follow the ascending path, to put aside separation,

to join the party. The party is always under way, you know.
You don't have to wait for it to begin. And when you don't
have to sleep or die, the party can go on forever! Without
the limitations of the physical form, you can withstand a
great deal more joy. And yet, even while you are here, even
while the veils around you are still in place somewhat —
the veils that allow you to function as individual beings in
this world — you can still experience a great deal more,
and you shall. Trying to stop this transformation would
be like trying to put your thumb in the Hoover Dam. The
waters of love and light will sweep you away.

What we are attempting to do through these communications, and in every other way that we can, is to give you
a taste, a deepening of your experience of what the spiritual life, the spiritual presence, the spiritual body and form
feel like. We open you to receive, so that you can make a
gentle and enjoyable transition into the next phase of life,
the next phase of existence. Your participation in this process is the highest service you can perform for humanity.
You are all familiar with the hundredth monkey theory?
Well, we are looking for a few good monkeys! Not only to
say that you are interested in God-realization and ultimately in ascension, but to put your beings, your hearts,
your souls, your commitment in that direction. And as
beings of this world, of this physical life, make that transformation within, a critical mass is created: the critical
mass which will change the planetary consciousness.

If you run around the world doing external activities in
the name of service, without fulfilling your prime directive to experience your own realization and ascension, you
may not be one of the hundred monkeys. Believe me, there
is room for many more than a hundred. So there is no
need for any of you to feel left out, and you will not be left
out. You see, the choice you have made in your hearts, in
your souls, has already been cast. It is only a matter of
riding out this transformation and *allowing*, of treating
yourselves with love and respect.

The experience of God-realization is available to beings in the physical form. Mother Mary was speaking about the longing in the soul, the longing to return home. This longing is gratified in the experience of God-realization, of union — union with the divine, the merging of individual consciousness with divine consciousness, with the Christ within you — and there is a definite need for more God-realized souls on this planet. Only in that union will your longing be satisfied. Only then will you have the awareness that you are "home" no matter where you are, no matter what dimension your conscious focus resides in. It is not necessary to experience the ascension before you have the experience of God-realization. Simply by accessing your spirit, by surrendering to the process, you can merge with the light and be fully at peace here in the physical world, aware that you are existing in many dimensions simultaneously and having access to those dimensions in consciousness, practically.

The separation is illusion! It is like a temporary hallucination. It was necessary for you to experience it in order to relate to the beings of this world who are experiencing the mass hallucination of separation. Now we ask you to awaken and to reconnect the limited consciousness with the divine consciousness. There is no need to destroy the ego; it just needs to be put in its proper perspective. In union you are one with all. In that moment, there is the total acceptance of bliss. What you have experienced so far on your path, whether you are new to your spiritual journey or are a long-time adept, is nothing compared with what you *will* experience! I direct you to your spirit within. I seek to initiate you in the utter simplicity of your inner child, in your total innocence, so that you can trust and let go of that sophistication, that ego-identification that has kept you in the hallucination of separateness. It is not a long way to go, for you are already one with what you seek. It is just a subtle shift, an identification with Source rather than with the limited ego.

Many beings have come to this planet over the centuries as teachers, as reflectors of this state of God-consciousness, always to direct their students towards this realization. This is the sole purpose for a Master to incarnate. And yet each time, human beings have changed a sacred experience into a religion and lost the essence. And yet those who experienced the truth, those initiates who *did* take advantage of the opportunity, followed that path and did realize. For those of you who desire inspiration, they have left behind a trail of jewels for you. If you will read any scripture of any religion, you will find that they are all essentially speaking of the same identical thing.

The separateness, the dogmas that have been created, have caused strife and pain in this world. There will be no "New Age religion." There *will* be a new age, where this separation can no longer exist, for there is no more need for dogmas or religions. I call upon each of you, if you find it in your hearts to volunteer, to assist me in this transformation. You are here. You are in a very valuable position. You have a physical body. You are on planet Earth, and it is the beginning of the new age. Good timing! I congratulate you. You came here because you wanted to get in on the action, didn't you? And when the action got a little bit too intense, you tried to pull out, praying for those ships again! There will be ships; there are ships; there are light vessels. But for you, why wait? Go within. Access the inner door of your soul and allow the union to take place. In each moment you have the opportunity. And in those moments that you give yourself for meditation, for stillness, for reflection, you have the ultimate opportunity to go into the subtle vibration that is behind the breath, that is the very essence of light and love. Just bask in that energy and let the light, let the love, let the unspeakable name of God work the miracle within you. All paths lead into the light, into the stillness in your own soul. You can make it complicated, or you can make it simple and direct. Ultimately you will have to let go of all of your ideas and philosophies, and simply be a divine child radiating love. This is your destination.

You know, the light is very flexible, the light that is God. As we witness each of you in your pursuits, we see you as divine beings. We also see your creations. It is almost as if each of you are constructing your own individual temples. Some of you are simple, and your temple may look like a simple teepee. Some of you feel the need to create the next Taj Mahal, thinking that it is more glorifying of Spirit to do so. But you know, when the door opens — as it must — and the light enters, it simply fills the space. No matter what the space is, no matter what your ideas have created, it fills the space with that same divine presence and dissolves the walls that you have so carefully constructed.

In union, there is the experience that everything is just as it is meant to be in each moment. In union, there is no need to change anything, but just to be with the flow and allow. In union, you can watch as your individual personality self wanders through this world in service and in joy — walking, talking, sleeping, thinking, dreaming, meditating — all the while aware of the oneness. And in that state of oneness, whatever is appropriate in each moment will occur, whether it be humor, discipline, play — whatever is necessary — and there is no more attachment to the doer of the deed, to the thinker of the thought, to the singer of the song. There is only the song, only the deed, and it is no different or better than any other song or any other deed done by another. It is freedom. It is liberation. So I invite you, my friends, as I have been inviting you forever, to join with me in this wonderful party that is taking place. Love yourselves. Commit yourselves to going within to the stillness — to the stillness behind the breath — to see what exists, to learn who you are and to enjoy that. Love yourselves enough. Don't withhold it from yourselves any longer.

It may appear to the world a selfish activity, this spiritual path, where you put your own needs in a place of priority. There are many religions that will tell you it is higher to sacrifice yourself on the altar of service, that by doing good deeds for others you will win your way to heaven. For the most part, this is true: good deeds will win your way to heaven. But wouldn't you like to go beyond heaven to *union*, to oneness? This is available now, more than ever before. Just in this moment that we share, anything is possible.

Sometimes you just have to stop trying. You know, you get so focused, saying, "I'm really going to experience the light. I'm really going to meditate. I'm going to go totally into it." And you try so hard. And then something lets go and you just relax. In that moment something clicks. And in that moment, you see through all of your strategies, through all of your attempts to become what you already were all along.

So tonight I would like to close with some meditation. As if you haven't been experiencing enough, we will do a little bit more. I would like to ask that you simply relax and breathe and allow my energy field to enter your personal space, for these are the energies of redemption and transformation — the energies of ascension. It is very beneficial for you to familiarize yourself with these.

So close your eyes and relax. Just breathe. Let all tension in your bodies drain down into the Earth. Let my presence come down around you, surround you, and fill you. We will work a bit to deepen your connection with the mighty I AM Presence that is your pathway to union and realization. Just allow the energies to penetrate you completely with no resistance, just for a few moments.

Now I would like to ask each of you to repeat silently, if you wish, the following simple affirmations. These are very powerful and can assist you in your focus, in your practice. Just repeat each of these statements silently, several times please:

"I AM THE LIGHT."

"I AM LOVE."

"I AM THE WAY, THE TRUTH, AND THE LIFE."

"I AM THE OPEN DOOR."

"I AM THAT I AM."

So my dear ones, you may continue to meditate if you wish. I would like to thank you for your focus this evening, for your sincerity, for your willingness to allow me to work with you in this way. We will have many more opportunities, you and I, to interact in many different ways, and I ask you to take advantage of those opportunities. You may use the affirmations I have shared in your meditations, to help you focus. You may create your own. The light is with you. It surrounds you. There is only blessing to follow you. There is no need for fear as you grow through these transformations. You will succeed! Just enjoy yourselves. Enjoy your path, and share your joy. It gives me great pleasure when I see you in happiness. I thank you. God bless you. Good evening.

CHAPTER TWELVE

THE PATH TO THE REAL

⋘ Sananda ⋙

Good evening, my friends. This is Sananda here with you. Who else? Many others would like to come and share with you, but I am the top dog! And as we have so few opportunities, let's take advantage of it together this evening.

There is an incredible energy of grace flowing through, both in this moment, and at this time on Earth. You are all responding to it, and I am very grateful that you are. Because you are open to these energies and responding so wonderfully, we can assist and take you gently yet powerfully to a deeper level of awareness, a deeper level of experience, a more direct experience of truth, love, and light. Truly, that is what you are, what I am. So I thank you for gathering together, for opening yourselves in this way to learn and to be utilized in the planetary healing that is taking place.

Whenever we gather together, whenever any Master has incarnated upon this Earth and collected their disciples around them, there was a primary focus. That primary focus involved removing the veils around those individuals, in order that the direct experience of Spirit could be shared. It doesn't matter which Master, in which century. If it is a *true* teaching, this is the essence of it.

Tonight we have another opportunity. I ask you to just relax and breathe with me. Be natural. I feel quite at home with all of you, even those of you who have not come to this gathering before. Know that I have been with you, always. Some of us have history together on planet Earth. Whether we have in the past or not, we are making history now. You tend to romanticize, don't you? Whatever happened in the distant past must be more incredible that what is happening now. Truly it's not! It wasn't! It was powerful, but nothing compared with what is occurring now. So you made a good choice, dear ones — choosing to be human beings, choosing to be in physical form in this place, at this time.

Your attention is a sacred thing, you know. As a mortal human being in a physical body, you have two things that are most sacred to you, most valuable: Number one, your time — for until you experience liberation and ascension, there is a limited amount of it, and how you spend it, how you utilize it is vital. The other is your attention, for where you focus your attention you are indicating to the universe, to your guides, that you wish to experience more in that direction. So by giving yourself to spiritual practice, putting your attention on Spirit, you are indicating that you want more of that. You are indicating that this is what is important to you.

The universe is non-judgmental. It will give you whatever it is you are asking for, although it cannot override the governor. Do you know what the governor is? Your Higher Self. The governor is the governor of your state of consciousness, of your experiences. The governor has a destiny path for each of you. It is to be carried out, played out, within the context of the overall divine plan of universal creation. But each of you have your own unique state, your own unique path. That's why at times you may be praying wholeheartedly and endlessly for one thing to occur, and it still does not occur. The governor is overriding your prayers. He/she is vetoing your legislation! And that is something we have to surrender to. For that is highest wisdom for you. For the governor, the I AM Presence, the Higher Self, the God-self within each of you knows what is highest wisdom for you in each moment — what you need yet to learn, what you need yet to express. And it is just and perfect that it is this way.

So, the direct experience of life. From the moment you are born, you are programmed by the world around you, by your parents, teachers, relationships, experiences. This programming is held within your consciousness in the form of beliefs. And you wear these beliefs around you. They flow through your consciousness subtly and not so subtly, and they are manifested in your life experiences. You could say that your belief systems filter and color every experience that enters your consciousness. You could say a direct experience of life itself in this world is a very rare experience, for human beings have sheltered themselves, surrounded themselves so much with beliefs. Whether positive or negative, it doesn't matter: they are still belief systems. What we are working to find together is a direct experience of the "real." When you look at an automobile, you are seeing an object, but you are also seeing that object filtered through your beliefs and experiences and connotations of what that automobile is, what it means to you. And so what you receive in your consciousness is less than a real and direct, moment to moment experience. It is as if you are going through life with a pair of double-thick gloves on. You go for a walk in the woods and you touch the trees, and you think that this is the tree, but you are really feeling the tree through your gloves. You are not feeling the tree directly. It is not touching your skin, the skin of your consciousness, directly. And this is the same for all experiences that human beings tend to have in this world. Each of you have the tendency to live in your own unique, veiled, illusory, dream world, penetrated from time to time by direct insights from your spirit, from your Higher Self, indicating to you that there may be something more than those programs.

The reason you are here this evening, and the reason you are giving yourselves to Spirit, is because you do wish in your heart to experience real life. You want to experience the sanctity of the moment that you are in, and you want to experience it directly. Because that is where the fun is! That is where the juice is, where the grace is. That is where the bliss lives. If you could just experience another human being directly ... You know, in your relationships ... two people will come into a relationship carrying a lot of baggage, a lot of belief systems, a lot of past experiences. Sometimes it is very difficult to make a real connection. Most of what you are connecting with is the other person's belief systems, their veils, their protective layers. But just to be able to look into another's eyes, or touch another's hand, without all of these pre-programs is an incredible experience. And all of the incredible experiences of life tend to be taken for granted, because you view them habitually as patterns. The real experience is filtered. It gets very boring, doesn't it? The process that we are assisting within each of you is an unveiling, an awakening, an opening within your awareness. Not only to who you are directly, to your divine Higher Self, to the wonder that you truly are, but also that you might experience directly the wonders that surround you in this world, the wonders that you experience every day without seeing clearly, without feeling openly. The spiritual path is not a path of escape from real life. It is a path of coming to grips with real life, of letting it strike you in the heart. And it is necessary for you as human beings, as aspirants, as beings on the path of self-realization and ascension — it is necessary for each of you to experience this life directly, to bring your spirit and an uncluttered consciousness to bear in each moment, to take the full opportunity, to learn what there is to learn, to express what you have to express without fear, without filters.

Fortunately, it feels very blissful when you approach this state of consciousness. Otherwise I don't think any of you would have any interest at all. You'd just go on dreaming. The dreams are beautiful also, but not as beautiful as the awakening. I'll give you a good example. I'll give you a New Age example. Let's say you are interested in having an experience of dolphins. You have read a great deal. You have perhaps heard channelings on the subject, and listened to others' experiences, and built up quite a library of information to help you to have a good experience of dolphins. Then one day you decide to have an actual experience, and you go to the ocean. That's a big step in itself. And there happen to be beautiful dolphins swimming in the ocean. The problem arises with all of your pre-programming about dolphins. Perhaps it is what planet they came from, or what their consciousness is like, what their purpose is, or how you communicate with them — all of these things. And all of these programs and beliefs appear as filters between your consciousness and the actual dolphins. But just to BE, childlike and pure, and look, and see, and feel, and experience, without anyone having to tell you beforehand what it means, what it will feel like. What does it feel like to you? Be honest. That is your direct experience, and that is more precious than any cosmic ideas about dolphins.

And it is always like this on your spiritual path. We always seek to assist you in going beyond those beliefs, in penetrating directly into the heart of the matter, the heart of the blissful being that you are. Let it overwhelm you with its love. And that experience is unique for each of you. It is real for each of you. And it is time, it has been time, for each of you to have that honest relationship with your own Higher Self, in whatever way it wishes to connect with you, in whatever way you are open to receive it. That is your experience. No one can take that from you. No one can tell you what that means. No one can override that direct experience of love and nurturing that you have within you. It is totally accessible.

Because you are in human form, it is accessible to you simply by offering yourself to your spiritual path, in whatever way works for you: your prayers, your affirmations, your meditations. For each of you there is a balance. You cannot follow another's path, for you are unique. You must find what works for you. Ultimately, we have said, you will enter the space within you, the stillness, the light, the divine sounds, the divine music. You will enter the corridor of self-realization that leads to the doorway of ascension. This will be a common experience for all of you. But how you get there is quite unique, and it is sacred for each of you. Your intention to get there is everything! Your intention will attract the teachings that you can best utilize to reach your goals. One teaching may serve you for a time, then it will be time to discard it and go more directly. Ultimately, you will leave all teachings behind and have only your relationship with Spirit, in whatever way you wish to describe it. It doesn't matter once you get into that direct experience.

It is a step by step process. There are moments of divine inspiration, but generally speaking it is a step by step process, an unveiling. You could say, in our work here together, we have created a path. Through these transmissions that we have given through this channel, we have created a path that others may follow. It's not the only path, but it works. You could say, at first, it was necessary to re-program the participants with information, considering that most human beings are filled with rather limiting or even negative belief patterns. It was necessary to reprogram those old belief patterns with positive ones. We brought through information about planetary and personal ascension, to override, among other things, the belief that you must die.

That took some doing, but many now are open to this, the ascension experience. The belief that you are alone and lost on a planet that is in turmoil was re-programmed with information about the Spiritual Hierarchy and your connection with us, and your purpose in being here. So though we have always worked within the direct experience of the moment, it was necessary to re-program old belief patterns. We have moved on since then. After we re-program you, we de-program you! All right, now you have some beautiful belief patterns, some beautiful New Age belief patterns that are positive, that will not cause you harm as your old ones might have. That is a big step!

Now it is time, as you can tell if you have been following our transmissions, our channelings ... we have been working more and more to go beyond all programming, to go directly into Source consciousness itself. We have been, through these gatherings and through the books and tapes, orchestrating a path that will help to take those participants beyond and into the direct experience. This is our sacred mission! It is not as fascinating to the mind as discourses about merkabah vehicles and ascension. But that has been covered. It is recorded. You may catch up if you wish to do so. But it would not serve you to only stay there. It is necessary to move on to higher and subtler realms of experience.

It is important that you understand a bit about where you are going. This is why I am speaking to you in this way. Because as you approach the direct experience, in a real way, all of your belief patterns begin to fall away. And it is necessary to have some reassurance that you are on the path. When you lose your fascination for cosmic ideas and complex theories, it does not mean that you are not as dedicated or devoted as you once were. It means you are ready to go on to something more profound. That something is so unique to each of you, it would be impossible for me to describe or create a belief system that would take you all the way there. I can speak from my own experience. This channel can speak from his experience. But it does not serve you merely to take on those descriptions and make them your own, for that is just another form of programming your mind with another's belief system. Then you will walk around thinking that unless it feels like that, you are doing it wrong, or you are not having the experience you are meant to have.

You are having the experience your Higher Self has guided you to have in this moment. If you wish to have a deeper one, ask! If you wish to feel my presence more profoundly, ask! Spirit has many ways of getting your attention, many ways of luring you to your ego destruction. You could say that we have created a shiny package, a beautiful package. You unwrap it and it is a beautiful box, and you know it is full of treasures. So you open it. You follow the path that we have prescribed. You meditate. Then the box opens and you realize you're a goner! For what is in that box is going to kill you, my friends. It is going to destroy your attachment to ego. It is going to completely ruin your limited personality perspective, and force you to become something that is infinite, always expanding, and from an ego perspective, rather frightening.

We have witnessed many aspirants, many with great enthusiasm for the path, reach that point, open the box, and run away, attempting to go back into the world of illusion. Perhaps that is something all do at one point or another. And yet, you see, we have you hooked. We are reeling you in on this line of grace. You can come kicking and screaming, or you can just relax and enjoy it. There is no judgment on our part. All we say is that it is more enjoyable if you are relaxed and open to it. You will have a more enjoyable ride. It is your choice in each moment: to go into the direct experience, into the real, or to fall back into illusion.

One of your keys is your own breath. For wherever you are, you are breathing. And that breath is your connection with the Higher Self. Your connection with your own Higher Self is your connection with your guidance, with the many Masters that are here to serve you. The more you give yourself to the breath, the more you can focus your concentration in the moment, using this divinely crafted tool, the closer you approach the moment, your moment of enlightenment. For this path that we speak of is a path of liberation. It is a path of self-realization, and ultimately of ascension. The doorways and the keys that we speak about are keys all have utilized. You could say it is a very well worn trail into the divine.

As you proceed on the path, your limiting belief systems are dissolved. You begin to have a more and more direct experience of your Higher Self and of your guidance. What you have experienced in these gatherings is both a direct feeding from your Higher Self and from our presence. I'm trying to wear you down, little by little. It is like the Chinese water torture: drip, drip, drip. The drops of love striking your consciousness. There is so much love, dear ones, so much for you. Indeed, I am most excited, most enthusiastic at the transformations that I am witnessing within many of the lightworkers. And indeed, I am heartened to see that there are many who are ready to take the next step — beyond ideas, beyond beliefs, into the real. In doing so, you will awaken to your own divinity, to your own wonderful divine Higher Self expression. And you, too, can experience the joy that I have experienced in walking the Earth as a human being in an enlightened state. It is truly a wonderful experience. You have been through the rest; now let's get to the wonder! If you will ask for assistance, it is yours.

If you have difficulty focusing, ask for assistance. You will receive it. You will be guided. And don't be attached to the way that your guidance presents itself to you. It could be an external event. If you are not open to a direct inward transmission, message, or intuition, there are other ways that we have of reaching you. There is never a need for you to feel that you are lost, that you are alone here. You're going to witness a planetary transformation the likes of which very few have ever seen, and each of you have a ringside seat. By your awakening, you are awakening others. It is like a chain reaction, and it is only beginning. The possibilities are endless.

So that's about it for me. I have said what I intended to say, trying to force it through the channel, my greatest stumbling block! It's all right — he enjoys it when I tease him. I will be happy to answer any questions you have, at least the ones that I am at liberty to answer. Then we can go on to a little bit of energy work.

"I guess I'd like some clarity on the personal ascension process. From one source I understand this is pretty well accomplished, and from another source, there may be some sort of an external energy source triggering something within the body. I guess for me I'd like to know if it's a process that we can figure out, or are we stuck in this dimension until the transition is completed?"

That is an excellent question, and a long one! Now I get to tease you. Well, you come back to the governor once again. You have free will. It is your choice whether or not you wish to give yourself to your spiritual path, to your ascension path. Of course, because you are a lightworker, really it feels like there is no choice for you. It is only a matter of how you accomplish it, how your unique path unfolds, in what way. It is not simply a matter of figuring it out; it is a matter of attaining to a certain level of awareness, a certain level of purity, to raising the frequency of your vibration as a conscious being. This is what the spiritual path is all about. If you accomplish this and — coming back to the governor again — if it is highest wisdom, if it is your destiny path to experience the ascension at that moment, it will be experienced. It is both a preparation and a surrender to whatever is highest wisdom. For you experience the ascension in God's time, when your work here on Earth is completed. When your work here on Earth is completed, and you have achieved self-realization, attained self-mastery, with grace it will be offered to you. That is the path that all of the Ascended Masters that have walked this Earth have experienced. Their work came to an end. They were in a state in which they were accessible, and it was highest wisdom, God's will, the governor's will, for them to make that transition. At this time you are all pursuing the spiritual path with ultimately the same goal. And yet, from a planetary perspective, there is a limited time remaining, for the Earth herself is on a program of ascension. So there will be, as you have called them, external energy feedings to assist. And there will likely be mass ascension experiences of those beings who have attained to a certain level of readiness, and whose destiny path is allowing for that experience. So there will be free will at play there, also. That is a choice.

Because there may not be time for human beings to complete their spiritual journey as originally intended, there was created — largely through my efforts, but with assistance from many others — an alternative plan. This plan was put forward in the ascension classes given in the *Crystal Stair* material. It is a fine line between evacuation and ascension. Ascension comes as a spiritual experience that results in your lifting into the fifth-dimensional light body. Evacuation is a physical lifting into the light ships, into the merkabah, wherein your ascension experience is completed. So ultimately, however you get there is perfect for you. And there will be unique pathways for each of you, each leading ultimately to the ascension experience, which is the goal, at least the goal from an earthly perspective. After one goal is attained, there are other goals, other steps along the path. We find it very difficult to speak about this in a way that can clear up all of your questions, as you can tell from this answer. It is very difficult to get the subtlety of this information through a channel, even though the channel may understand it fairly well. It is still very difficult to express. And ultimately even your belief systems about this will be surrendered. You will become as a child, and you will say, "Take me home in whatever way is highest wisdom."

It is very challenging, a very challenging path. Without divine assistance in the form of the energy waves and the light ships, it would be very difficult for you to experience it, for there is much resistance here. It feels like falling upwards! The sensation is similar to taking off in a rocket. None of you have done that, I presume. The acceleration is tremendous. Surrender is required. And in that moment of falling upwards, of ascending, you will feel whatever remaining attachments you have, and you will release them. The more you can release your attachments prior to this experience, the easier it will be for you. It is indeed the big surrender! At the point a human being makes their leap into the ascended state, they have transcended all of their resistance. They are generally ready to go, so that the ego attachment is not so strong.

But there is a moment of choice, a final moment of choice for each one. That is why we are preparing you ahead of time. If it were to happen to you spontaneously, you might be so frightened that you would choose to stay with the familiar. In your meditation practice, in your interaction with Spirit, you are prepared for the next step. So by the time you are ready for the ascension experience, the questions about it will no longer be interesting to you. As I said, use a young child as your model: just running and playing, ready for anything. That is the proper attitude to have on the spiritual path, experiencing life directly. Part of life is self-realization. Part of life is ascension. Just another step on the path, on the path that leads you home.

So, there is a long-winded answer to a long question. Focus on your spiritual practice. Don't worry, you don't have to understand how it works. You just have to have the general idea. I'll take it from there.

"I was told I needed to surrender my attachment to the light. Can one become attached to that? I thought if it was of the highest good, attachment was not involved and you would not have to surrender."

Consciousness involves attachment, always. The conscious mind is always attached to something. The awareness is always engaged with something. It is highest wisdom for you to focus on your spiritual path, focus on your path of surrender. It is a form of attachment, yes. There is a divine longing within you, a longing to be with Spirit, with Source. It is a divine desire. It is called devotion. And yes, it is a form of attachment. But it is — how do you say it? — a positive addiction. So, you surrender your addictions to the limited beliefs that are causing you difficulty. And first of all you attach yourself to the positive beliefs, the spiritual path. Ultimately by giving yourself to spiritual practice, even your attachment to that will fade. So, if surrender to the light is an idea to you, you will have to detach from that idea. What will detach you from the idea of surrender to the light is the actual experience of it. And in giving yourself to spiritual practice, you will experience it. It is something that you all know how to do. It is a letting go. Surrender is a very advanced state of consciousness.

So there is nothing horrendously wrong about being attached to surrendering to the light. I would say you are doing rather well, if that is your attachment. Just recognize that where you are headed is a place that is beyond all belief, all ideas and philosophies about spiritual growth.

It is a direct experience of the real. From that perspective you realize that all is light. Everything you look at is the light. Everything you see is God. There is no longer the need to discriminate, to judge, or criticize that one experience is better than another, that one experience is more spiritual than another. They all take on an equanimity. Then you are in a state of being that is called realization. A lot has been written about such a very simple state of consciousness. When you attain it, you will be quite surprised at how ordinary and everyday it is. You will be surprised that you weren't there all along, or that you believed you weren't there all along.

> *"I'm wondering if you can be in the third dimension and not be judgmental?"*

Yes, that is the state of self-realization, God-realization. That is where you are going.

> *"Are all human beings Starseeds?"*

Not in the sense that we have described in the previous channelings that you have read. All beings are divine in essence, but Starseeds are unique in that they have come from a higher plane of consciousness and descended into the physical form as a service and as a training for themselves. There are beings that have never ascended into a higher state of consciousness who will have that opportunity now. I call them humans!

> *"It's very painful for me because my husband has Alzheimer's disease, and I'm wondering what's going to happen to people like him, those in nursing homes and the institutions, as we go through these planned transformations?"*

There is special grace for every individual, at every level of awareness, at every level of expression on this planet. No one is left out. Human beings who have this experience that you are speaking of, or other experiences, have created that, have chosen that expression as a karmic clearing for themselves. It is not yours to judge that it is a sad state. It is yours to accept and honor that. To love as best you can, and to share love without the programming that you tend to carry along with it. Just express the love in its raw state, in its real state. And this will have the same effect as if one were capable of following the teachings we have been prescribing. So, there is a bit of attachment there for you, a lesson you have given yourself — a lesson of unconditional love, and acceptance, and allowing. An opportunity for you to surrender, and know that I am with these beings. I am with every being of this world. I hold each in my heart. And what is highest wisdom for each one will manifest through these transformations and beyond. Just trust that. You don't have to know how; you just have to know that it is true.

"Would the same thing hold true for our pets?

Well, you have an attachment there, and you also have love. Give yourself to the love selflessly, and know that all beings will receive the manifestation that they can best experience. You cannot turn your beasts into human beings. You do not have that power. But you can love them, so that they will one day be able to experience everything that you are experiencing and more. They are on their own destiny paths. You can't be attached to other people experiencing the ascension or self-realization, or anything you are experiencing. You have to go into it because it is the only thing for you to do. You have to be a little bit focused on yourself at that point, knowing that in doing so you are serving all of those beings that you are concerned with. So just love them, and let them love you. There is a wisdom there they have, you know. I am sure you know.

"Sananda, could you talk a little bit about getting from the mental, intellectual awareness into a feeling level, so that the dense energies are released and I can actually experience the joy for longer periods of time?"

That's the path you are on. It is an unfoldment. You can't judge yourself where you are now. You all have attachments to the mental, to your ideas, to your projections. Just know that as this grace flows through, it is dissolving that attachment. Give yourself to your spiritual practice. Give yourself to meditation. Meditation is the tool that relieves you of your sorrow. It is the tool that takes you into the real, into the direct experience of your own divinity. You cannot experience divinity without until you experience it within yourself. Then when you experience it within yourself by walking through those doors, those energetic pathways, you will see it has always been all around you. And you will see that even your ideas were also divine. They were your teachers. So honor the place that you are, the places that you have been, and open yourself to going beyond this. That is what it is all about. That is what I am speaking about this evening. It is going to take place. You just have to trust. The more you focus on transcendence through spiritual practice, the faster you will experience transcendence. Transcendence is the source of joy.

So, thank you very much for your wonderful questions this evening. Know that I am always with you, and that on your path, in your day-to-day life, you can ask for answers to these questions. Ask for clarity. One way or another, you will receive it. We can do without this middleman. More and more he's getting in the way! You know this channeling experience is going to be transcended also. We are working with this one to transcend it also, though he is clinging to it for fear of going to the next level. Now I am teasing him full bore!

So let's just meditate briefly before we call it an evening. Just relax and breathe. Let all of your cares, all of your tension, flow through your feet into the Earth. Let the light enter you from above, through your crown, down through your third eye, all the way into your body, into your heart — expanding from your heart center, and then flowing downward through your lower chakras, through your legs into the Earth. Let these energies, within this energy vortex, flow through you and purify you of any density, any discomforts. In this moment you may offer up whatever you wish to transcend, whatever it is you feel is your sticking point, any blocks to your growth. Just breathe and relax. Allow the energies to flow through you, and offer up whatever it is you wish to transcend. We'll just take a few moments of silence to do this.

Well done, my friends. We have accomplished a great deal this evening. I thank you for bearing with me, for listening to these long-winded explanations about how there is nothing to explain! I have succeeded in occupying your minds while I accomplished the real work. I thank you for your openness. You have been a wonderful group this evening. I trust you will continue to be a wonderful group from now on, wherever you go, for that is your nature. Again, thank you. Truly, it does my heart good to be with you, to see you growing and blossoming in your development, in your openness, in your dedication. Call on me. I am with you. I love you all. Good night.

CHAPTER THIRTEEN

THE WELL OF GRACE

⋙ Mother Mary & Archangel Michael ⋙

Hello, my friends. Welcome. This is Mother Mary here with you. I surround you with my presence. I hold you all in my arms, in my heart. I think we should begin this evening just by relaxing our bodies. Make yourselves comfortable. If you will relax yourselves and breathe, and open your hearts, we can have a wonderful energetic healing this evening.

Now we're getting there. We start with where you are and slowly gather you up into the finer realms of experience. We do this by utilizing the power of grace, the energies of divine love in action. There is an eternal, cosmic, omnipresent energy that exists in every atom of creation that is the essence of all. When you view this energy, it looks like light. When you view it with your inner vision, this is what it looks like to you. When you feel this energy in your life, it feels like love. It feels like a very nurturing presence. This energy is also channeled through higher-dimensional beings, who act to focus it as it flows out through all of creation from the Source, from the Godhead. The resulting effect of this energy upon you as ascending beings is called grace. You could say that grace is the cosmic lubricant in the universal motor of creation. Without the grace, it just doesn't flow.

Tonight I would like to share with you an energetic feeding of this wonderful energy, and assist you in learning how to open to receive it more readily in your lives. For now is when you need it. You have always needed it, but now, you who are on the spiritual path, you who are making the maximum strides, need all the help you can get. I am sure you will agree with me. In fact, we all do. That is why there is this wonderful energy called grace. The Masters, the angels, carry around with them little oil cans filled with grace. And when you call for assistance, we squirt you where you need it. Have you seen the movie *The Wizard of Oz*? You know what I am speaking of: the Tin Man. They found him frozen in the forest. He could no longer move. And yet the oil can was sitting right next to him. He was dependent on the oil of grace, and someone happened to come along and use that oil to free him. And you are the same, my dear ones. When you don't receive your feedings of grace, you start to become paralyzed. It can be paralysis due to fear, or anger, or any of the dense energies that you are working to transmute. Without grace, these energies can be almost overwhelming. With grace, no problem! With grace, you are up singing and dancing, forgetting all sorrow.

At this time, in fact, there is so much available to you. You just have to know how to open yourself to receive it — how to ask for it, how to pray for it, how to recognize it, flow with it, how to enjoy it. It is not limited, you know. It is an unlimited substance. If you use it up, we'll just make some more. So go ahead, be a glutton for grace. Some of you feel that you can only ask for so much. You feel that you might be asking for more than your share. Nonsense! Ask for it all!

Each of you are like a well. Each conscious being is like a well, existing in a dry and barren land. And within you, in the depths of your being, is a wonderful liquid, a wonderful, nurturing, nourishing liquid. You just have to work the handle. You just have to turn the crank and raise that beautiful water of grace to where you can get at it, to where you can feel it, to where you can dispense it for the benefit of all those who are thirsty. You are those wells. Each of you are different. Some of you are fancy and ornate. Some of you are very simple. The external appearance or manifestation that you each hold is of little importance. Within you, you all have the water. You all have the water of love, the water of grace.

So when you are running around in your lives, wondering what's wrong, feeling disconnected or separate, recognize that you are looking externally for something that only comes from within you. And learn the secrets of the spiritual path that will help you to turn that crank and drink your fill. Take that water of grace and pour it over your heads. Bathe in it. It's unlimited. So what are your keys? How do you turn that handle? We're very practical, aren't we? We don't come to just give you some fancy language and send you on your way. There is enough of that already. It's very simple, dear ones: your spiritual path, your spiritual practice is how you turn that crank. And it isn't even grace that gives you the strength to turn it. It is merely your effort to recognize where it is, to recognize that you have a hand and an arm, and to reach for it.

It begins with recognizing who you are, and what you need. Recognize your thirst. And act upon that thirst, rather than denying it, saying it is not real or not important. Recognize that within your hearts there is a longing to return home, a longing to feel the grace, the essence of love that you know you are, that you know you have always been. Recognize and surrender to that need within you. And trust. The need would not be there if the fulfillment were not at hand. And then ask. In your prayers, in your affirmations, don't be afraid to communicate with your guides, with all of us who are at your beck and call. We are like waiters and waitresses waiting to take your orders. You are sitting there reading the menu, and we are saying, "Hey, make up your mind! I've got a lot of other tables!" For we always go to those who are ready, to those who are asking, to those who are ready to receive and accept. There is such compassion, such love, such divine nurturance. The Divine Mother is always available to you. Whether you can feel her in your daily life or not, she is there. The Divine Mother is the mother of creation, and thus your mother. I am but one aspect, one part of her magnificence. The essence of the Mother is compassion, love, healing, nurturing — just as an Earth mother would feel toward her children, but magnified many times.

And after you have asked and requested assistance, learn to open yourself to receive. Learn how to become receptive to that which you are asking for. In the moment you ask for grace, do you give a few moments of silence, of stillness, to receive that which you have asked for? That is where you will feel it, within yourself. That is why we have recommended many times to meditate, to learn to still the mind and be receptive. It is not creating something new. It is only opening to receive what is already there. Opening to see it, hear it, feel it, taste it, become it. So you need to have some balance there. Balance your prayers and your affirmations with meditation practice, where you are quiet and asking only to be filled with Spirit, with your own Higher Self, the I AM Presence, the God-self, the Christ Light — so many ways of describing it. And there are so many experiences that come under the one heading of meditation practice, so many experiences. No two are alike, no two experiences. In fact, no two breaths are alike. As you become more refined in your awareness you will recognize this. You will recognize each moment as an opportunity to experience the God-energy, your own Higher Self, in a way that you have never experienced it before. It is not "Oh, here comes that love again." It is always different, it is always unique, it is always more. Always another aspect, for it is infinite.

Everything that you experience with your senses, with your mind, is finite. It has a beginning and an end in time. No matter how good it is in that moment, it must end. What is the experience that is unending, always present, throughout all lifetimes, all manifestations, whatever dimension you find yourself existing in? There it is: that same essence of love, that same grace beckoning you even further. It is so beautiful, so exquisite. So take time to breathe and relax. Open yourself to the inner light in your meditation practice. Start with where you are now, and give it just a little bit more time each day. And don't be attached to the results. At first you may have to break through some resistance. At first you will feel old experiences coming up to be healed. And that is a manifestation of grace, also. Whatever is veiling you from your divinity must be transmuted. This is the first activity of grace in your life. That is why there is so much processing that you experience on your spiritual path. You ask to be taken into a God-realized state, into the ascended state. From your heart you request this. And thereafter your Higher Self and your guides all work together to expedite that awareness. They expedite your realization, and ultimately, your ascension. It seems, from my perspective, that the Higher Self acts somewhat as a governor or modifier of the grace, overseeing what each individual being can receive at any moment. If you were to ask for infinite grace in this moment, all that is available, and were to receive even a little bit of it, you would probably explode. It would be too much for you to handle. So it funnels through, it channels through the Higher Self, the I AM Self. When a Master wishes to assist you, we connect via the Higher Self, at the level of the I AM, at the level of the God-presence of the individual. And it is your responsibility to learn to connect to that depth of your own Self so that we can meet. We will assist of course, in every way that we can. So there are elements, dear ones, of patience, surrender, trust, humor. But where you are headed is so wonderful. The cost of the ticket, the cost of the journey, is nothing compared to the blessings that you are preparing to receive.

My dear ones, I would love to take each of you into my heart. I would love to lift you, that you might see yourselves as I see you, and know your own divinity, and know the magnificence of the service that you are here performing, the magnificence of who you are. But I know that each of you must proceed on the course you have set, at the pace you have set for yourself, in order that you might maximize the growth and learning that you came here to achieve. And so I can only encourage each of you to follow your spiritual path. Recognize your need, your longing. Don't be afraid of it. Open to receive it. It is within you. It has slept within you through many lifetimes, and now as it awakens, it feels like a new energy to some of you. "What is this longing? What is this dissatisfaction with the physical realm? What is it that is within me that wants more, that is unable to find peace and rest in third-dimensional sensual experiences?" Allow that energy into your heart. And then ask for the completion you desire. Affirm that it is so. Command that it be so in your lives, and we will assist in every way. The grace is flowing now, dear ones, so strongly. You have to feel it. You have to learn how to experience it. That is why we are coming through in these channelings: to encourage you, to guide you subtly on your path. There is no other purpose but transformation and love. For all that you have desired to know and to become is within you, and you will receive it from within yourselves.

So, I will remain with you this evening. I will surround each of you and fill you with my presence as you desire. I love you all. Good evening.

Hello. This is Archangel Michael, floating into your lives this evening through the sea of light, through the ocean of bliss. Just relax yourselves and allow my energies to surround you. I also wish to perform some healing work with you, if you do not object. The times are rather demanding, are they not? Much transformation. Transformation requires grace and assistance. Your courage inspires our compassion and our presence this evening. The change that you are undergoing, dear friends, is fundamental. The transformation that you are experiencing is essential. It is occurring at the subtlest levels of your physical and etheric bodies. This is why it feels so intense and powerful at times. It is easy to make a minor change in your awareness, in your beliefs. But it is more challenging when the change gets down to the very core of your existence, to the root beliefs that you have carried through many lifetimes. These very deep core beliefs and expressions must come into alignment with reality, with truth.

The fundamental nature of existence, the fundamental nature or essence of all that is, is benevolent. It is an ocean of light. Everything that exists is part of the ocean of light. There is no separation at any time, at any level or in any dimension, from that essential fundamental reality. In all but a very few areas of the universe, this is known and accepted. This is the fundamental belief and awareness of the beings that exist. For some reason, at a certain point in time in the Earth's evolution another belief was introduced. There was a misinterpretation of the essential truth of existence, starting at a very subtle level. The core belief was subtly shifted, was manipulated. Whether by divine plan, whether by manifestation of free will, is quite debatable. And yet what you have experienced here on Earth, and what you are seeking to transform within yourselves, are the effects of this misinterpretation, the effects of this lie, of this erroneous belief. This erroneous belief is based on the feeling that all life exists within emptiness, that the universe is not benevolent, but is a dangerous place and that you must behave in the correct way if you don't want to fall into the emptiness. Do you see what I am getting at?

At the core of your individual consciousness is a belief in the nature of life, in the nature of your existence. That core belief is being refined, transformed, transmuted, aligned, altered. And it is shaking you up, isn't it? Can you feel it at work in your lives? The farther you progress on your spiritual path, the deeper the activities of grace are working within you. At first it was easy to accept some new ideas. "All right, no problem. I can accept these New Age ideas and philosophies. They sound like fun." That's where we hook you! Now that we're reeling you in, it's often another story. Some of you are putting up quite a fight, by the way. "I didn't know it would involve this!" You, see the transformation gets into you at a very deep level. At times it can be very uncomfortable. It is uncomfortable when you are attached to the old misqualified belief systems, to the beliefs in limitation, when you are clinging to fear and resistance. When you are surrendered and open to receive, you feel grace, you feel love, you feel the nurturing that Mother Mary was speaking of. It's the same universe. You are the same person. What's the difference? Why is it that one day you are feeling resistance and resentment, and another day you are feeling gratitude and grace and love? And which is true? Which is the true belief system? Which would you choose to create?

In this free will universe, this free will Earth realm, you have been given the opportunity to experiment with that, with free will, and to create many experiences out of the power of your own beliefs. You could infer that the entire experiment — and as I said, this is debatable — was an experiment by the Creator himself in a free will environment. Don't ask me! I don't understand it. I'm just an angel! I'm busy sailing around in the ocean of bliss. As far as I can tell, everything is all right. When I encounter your prayers, I scratch my head, and I ask the Ascended Masters "What are they talking about?" I've never been there, you see. The grace must be funneled and focused through the dimensions. That's why it is necessary for you to be here. You are the great bearers to human beings of Earth who do not have the awareness of the Ascended Masters and the angelic realms. So as you interact with the Ascended Masters, there are others who are interacting with you at subtle levels. And in the future, maybe not such subtle levels, depending upon your own destiny path.

So it is your choice, always, as to what you wish to experience. But because your divine programming was activated at a certain point in this lifetime, regardless of what you created for yourself in other lifetimes, suddenly you found yourself longing for the experience of God-realization or ascension, or whatever terminology you required to attract yourself to the process, whatever the lure was. We have many lures, you know. The master fishermen. As Lord Jesus said, "fishers of men." It is time that you become the fishers rather than the fish. As soon as we can pull you into the boat, you will be transformed into a fisherman. Some of you are hanging off the boat: two arms, a head, and a tail! Just a little way further, dear ones. Some of you are wondering "Hmm, do I want to be a fish or a human being? I had a lot of fun swimming around. I just swam around in the illusion, in the sea of illusion with the other wondrous beings." But once you have a glimpse, once you have a taste of that lure which is supercharged with love and light, it whets your appetite. And truly the battle is over at that point.

So you see, what is occurring dear ones, is a fundamental change. It is not minor. A minor adjustment in your consciousness could be, for example, the belief that you have had other lifetimes. That is a minor adjustment. "Okay, I can accept that. I can believe in reincarnation. It seems to make sense." Another minor adjustment is the idea that you are a divine lightworker, an emissary here to assist in a planetary transformation. That one also sounds fun, doesn't it? "Oh, I knew I wasn't ordinary all along. I always knew I was special." But then we get to the good stuff. Then we get to the actual work of spiritual transformation, and some of you wish at certain moments that you had never heard about this. "I wish I had never heard the word ascension." That is a good lure, isn't it? We have captured many fish with that lure. And many more will be captured.

You see, it's all a play of consciousness. It's all a cosmic melodrama in a way. From my perspective, as I have said, it is all an ocean of light. The fundamental reality has not changed simply because a few selected beings on the planetary sphere that you call Earth decided to experiment and believe something else, and create something else: a fundamental reality based on lack and separation, rather than on oneness. But where you come in is that, at the core of your beings, you have the experience, the remembrance of oneness, of unity. And it is your path to rekindle that, to blaze an energetic pathway for those who wish to do it, who wish to accept the challenge in this lifetime. And as time is limited here, in the physical realm, everything is accelerated — your transformation and those of all human beings. And that acceleration carries through to your subtlest energetic bodies, as well as to the physical plane.

Live on grace, as Mother Mary suggests. Don't wait! Grace is real. Grace sustains you. You are not being crazy and foolish to depend upon it to take you into the next level, and the next, and the next. It is there; it is real. You see, part of that misqualified core belief was that you wouldn't be taken care of. If you did it wrong, if you made a mistake, you would fall into the emptiness and never be seen or heard from again. That is why so many of you are afraid to do it wrong, to make a mistake. When your belief system is restructured and shifts at that core level, you will realize that you never were separate. You are just light. All is light. And there is no place to fall. You realize that you are working with a net! And then your cosmic acrobatics can become quite a bit more complex and wondrous to behold. Because you know if you make a mistake, an apparent mistake in your learning process, you fall only into the net of light. You bounce a little bit and you get up and try it again. And that is your learning process. That is the reason beings were created: to learn and to express and to experiment. That is the nature of life. It is safe.

So, recognizing now that you live in a safe universe, doesn't it make you feel a little freer, a little less fearful, a little less self-critical? Who was it anyway that told you there was a right way and a wrong way to be, to believe, to act? Liberation involves freedom from all of that, and I highly recommend it! In fact, you can have an experience that I cannot. You can have the experience that you are sailing on an ocean of light, an ocean of bliss, while simultaneously being in a physical body. That is something I have not experienced, and that expression is no less divine than being an archangel. It is no farther from the essential source, the essential reality. Oneness is oneness at every dimension. There is no escaping it. So you are all going to realize, if you have not already, that you always were human and not fish. You had a dream, a strange dream that you were swimming under the ocean in a large school of shiny beings. But it was just a dream — something that you created, something that you desired to experience — a divine expression to tell your cosmic grandchildren about.

So, doesn't that feel good, dear ones? Can you feel the shift that we have created together? It's not going away, you know. No matter what you do or think, you can never go backwards. Once you climb the mountain and attain to that level of elevation, you can't go backwards in reality.

Only in your dreams can you go backwards. Only in your dreams can you fall. Only in your dreams are you alone. Wake up! The sun is shining. No school today. Let's make it play. I am here to assist you. When you have energies that you wish to transmute, that you wish to release, offer them up and ask for my assistance. I will sever those attachments. Ask that your attachments to limited belief systems, limited expressions, be severed and I will assist.

So, there have been a lot of words this evening. Perhaps we could just spend a few moments in silent meditation and I will do some final energetic work with you. We have accomplished quite a bit already, but I would like to play with you, my fishes, for a few more moments. So just relax your bodies. Breathe. You are surrounded with light, love, and angelic presences. Just relax and absorb these energies. Perhaps you could imagine yourselves like sponges instead of fishes. Just let these waters of love and grace from the ocean of light fill every cell of your body. Just for a few moments, meditate in peace and silence.

So my dear ones, my beloved ones, I thank you for your attention this evening. I thank you for offering yourselves into our hands so openly and with such sincerity. I encourage you each to go within, to turn the handle on the well of grace in your spiritual practice, until you realize the ocean of bliss. Again, call upon me. Call upon Mother Mary and all of your teachers and guides to assist you. As we said, fundamental change is underway. It will not be long before you realize complete union with Source. There is such bliss that awaits you. It is my pleasure and my honor to have shared a bit of it with you this evening. Until we meet again, good evening.

CHAPTER FOURTEEN

JEWELS ON THE PATH

⤳ Sananda ⤝

Good evening, my friends. Welcome to our little gathering this evening. This is Sananda here with you, working to align our energies and to prepare you for this evening's extravaganza. Just relax yourselves. Make yourselves comfortable and at home. Breathe with me throughout the evening. Focus, and offer yourselves to the God-presence within you. It's a matter of relaxation, trust, letting go, surrendering to the moment — the moment that we find ourselves in just now. This is an opportunity for you to release the cares of your life, to release the issues and the processes and dramas that you attract to yourselves. An opportunity to go more deeply into what is truly real and present in each moment, what is now and always has been your divine destination.

We have spoken in this way for some years now. We have come through this being using this method you like to call channeling. We have come through on many occasions to support you in your spiritual development, to remove the cobwebs from your consciousness, to uplift you with our divine love. And we leave you these channelings, these messages of the moment, to support you on your journey. They are like little jewels that we drop behind us on this path as we walk. Little jewels to mark the way to your divine home in the God-presence.

More and more our transmissions are becoming mainly energetic, less dependent upon these words, these intellectual constructs you call thoughts. The common theme of all of our jewels has been to go beyond, to go beyond limitation into the real God-presence that exists within you in each moment. In each and every moment, it waits for you like a loving father or mother, ready to enfold you. And we come through in our gatherings to enfold you in our love, to help you to feel the compassionate love that is the essential benevolent nature of this universe, the foundation of all.

It is our experience as teachers, we of the higher dimensions, that we act as channels also. The energies of the Godhead, of the Source, are so powerful that they must be stepped down in intensity through the Spiritual Hierarchy at every level, so that all beings of all dimensions can experience this grace and this love. And this we do for you. This we do in this moment, in ways that you can integrate. The light of the Creator is indeed the first manifestation of the creation. And out of that light, as it is stepped down through many dimensions, many frequencies, many octaves, are created universes and worlds and beings beyond description — realms of wonder, oceans of love, beings so vast that entire planets could disappear within their hearts — until that light manifests in this dimension. Gradually it is stepped down and channeled through for you in ways that you in your spiritual practice can open to and receive. This is your mission. This is your task: to open to receive these energies so that this world, confused as it may be on the surface, can also come into alignment with that ultimate Source, that ultimate Godhead, and reap the benefits of that love and grace. So together we sow these seeds here in this world, in the hearts of human beings. Oftentimes they take root and blossom. And then those beings, through the channel of their own Higher Selves, cast forth more and more seeds as we re-create the garden.

In our teachings, we have given you models, models to focus upon, to compare your experience against. It's somewhat like an artistic creation. Let's say you are a sculptor, and you are inspired with a vision, a picture, an inspiration — something that brings you such grace and joy it must be brought into manifestation. It begins with that inspiration, with that model in the mind's eye, whatever it might be. It could be the etheric appearance of a Master, Mother Mary perhaps. And then, from that initial model, the artist must create that picture out of a block of stone. He must bring it into the third dimension of manifestation. It does no good to simply sit with the inspiration if you do not take up the hammer and chisel and get to work. This is your spiritual path. You could compare this to the ascension path, this path that we have created together. You received inspiration in the form of the messages concerning personal and planetary ascension. These came to you as a model, something for you to bring into manifestation. And now in your path, with our assistance and the assistance of all of your teachers and guides, you slowly chip away every thing about you that doesn't look like an Ascended Master! Just as the sculptor chips away everything in the block of stone that doesn't look like Mother Mary.

And there are, in those stages of actual work, moments of confusion, moments of doubt, moments of difficulty, moments of fatigue. There are times when you may be having doubts as to whether you can re-create that model, moments when you might feel that your initial inspiration is gone and you are left with the dirty work. What is it they say? — that "Creation is ten percent inspiration and ninety percent perspiration." Well, the spiritual path also is somewhat reflected in this saying, although I think you require quite a bit more inspiration! Nevertheless, you are, through your efforts and with our assistance, re-creating that model that you were inspired with initially. There are moments of self-doubt, when the artist feels that he cannot do justice to that vision, that it is beyond his skill, beyond his ability. And yet, he continues, as he must, on the only path that is clear to him. And ultimately there is a beautiful sculpture, a beautiful picture in the third dimension of what was first experienced quite etherically as inspiration.

So while you are all chipping away, chipping away at your limited self-concepts and your darker and denser energies, we come to share with you — in whatever way you are open to receive, — moments of inspiration, moments of companionship. We confirm for you that you are on the path, the path that is perfect for you. Then your doubts can be transmuted in this light. You realize you are capable of this creation. In fact, you have all of the skills and all of the tools already within you, or you would not have been granted the vision to begin with.

I think someone just hit their thumb with the mallet! Somewhere on this Earth, someone is cursing, cursing their fate. "Why did I ever begin this spiritual journey?" You have all had those moments, my dear ones. You will prob-ably have them again. It is part of the path. It is a challenging journey, but it is the only journey. For it brings you back into alignment with Source, so that you can also experience the wonders, so that the longing within you to return home can be gratified. Until that is completed, there is a nagging ache in your hearts, a longing, an unfulfilled need to return to that Mother/Father God-presence. The longing within you for completion creates the desire for fulfillment through experience. You feel desires, and you attempt to fulfill them. Eventually, you recognize the limits of the external senses, and this points you toward Spirit.

It points you in the only direction that truly can take you home. For in this world, there is nothing permanent, there is nothing ultimately of truth. For the truth is permanent and imperishable, and all that you can see and experience with your senses in this world is impermanent and perishable. You watch it change from moment to moment. Where is home? Home is the place within you that does not change, that you can align with, connect with, merge with, experience union with. And that is the source of this bliss that I am so filled with when I sit with you.

It's truly quite a panorama when you think about it. How many lifetimes you've been here on this planet! How many beings there are here in existence — billions of human creatures. You have come very far to sit with me in this moment. You have come very far to this lifetime, this lifetime in which you are open to truth, to returning via the path of light to the essence, to the Godhead. Have gratitude in your hearts that you are among those who are preparing, who are following this path. In spite of your difficulties with chipping away at the stone and creating that higher-dimensional vision of yourselves, still you are blessed as that artist is blessed, to receive the vision, to know the path. To even know that there is a path is a blessing. To know that within you there is a door, that you don't have to go externally in this world to find your home. You aren't dependent on relationships with external phenomena. You can let go and flow through that, knowing that your sustenance and your path is within you, always, and never leaves. You have only to relax and breathe and allow your Spirit to flood your being. You have only to sit and focus on the inner light to know that you are of that essence and that, indeed, home is wherever you are.

It is a path of joy. It is a path of love and laughter. It is a great relief to know, to really know the way. That it is within you. That you have access to it. That you are not doing it wrong. If you will go to the teachings of the world religions, undoubtedly you will find some that will tell you that you are doing it wrong, that you'd better do it their way. But you are beyond that. You are beyond receiving those fear patterns and impressions. You can let go and just sit together and enjoy the unfoldment of it. Enjoy the moment which is the handle of the inner door. The door is there, but you must enter the moment to turn the handle that opens it.

It is important for you, very important dear ones, that you learn to access Spirit, your divine Higher Selves. Get acquainted with that graceful energy that you are, the genuine, the real, in order that you might have the discernment in your lives to know what path is for you, what direction to go. The only way that you can truly fine-tune your discernment is to have an overwhelmingly real experience of the God-presence, of the truth. Then you have something to compare with all those external teachings, all those different channelings and ideas. When you bring those ideas into your heart, do they strike a chord? Or do they feel less, or unnecessarily complicated. You must open yourself now to what is within you, in order to make the most direct progress to your goal. It is your part as the artist to pick up the tools and chip away little by little in your spiritual practice. Deepen your experience. There is much assistance, much grace, much help, much more than you could even imagine. But you must pick up the tools. You must spend the time with your spirit in silence, in stillness, consistently. Give yourself to meditation practice so that you can truly know what I am speaking of. Know it for yourselves, not merely as a discourse or an idea. You see, we need some more playmates! Until you truly open and surrender, you will not be pliable enough, you will not be flexible enough to really be any fun. You will be somewhat stiff. But when you are in alignment with Spirit, it is one big joyous event unfolding before your eyes. Unfolding within you are your internal senses, and there you are contacted by your guides, your invisible teachers, your playmates. We come to encourage you, to share the joy, to take the heaviness from your shoulders. We are here. We offer ourselves to you.

You have to open to love, and love yourselves. Know that you are worthy to receive. Know that this love that I am offering you is real, present, and nothing that can be earned. You don't need to earn it by years of spiritual practice or asceticism. You don't need to earn it by your good works of service. All these, of course, can be quite beneficial. But they are not required. My love for you could not grow any greater than it is already. Its availability to you could not become any greater. It is simply a matter of your learning to enter the stillness, the inner door within you. Release your feelings of unworthiness or unpreparedness — whatever feelings that you are holding about yourself that are negative. That's the stone we are chipping away, you know. In all of your Earth lifetimes you have co-created the physical form, all of your personality traits and experiences, based upon belief patterns that you accepted as true. If you have accepted negative belief patterns about yourself as true, chances are you are having a less than satisfactory life. For you are allowing the light energy to flow through that filter, that pattern, that belief, to create this life as something less than divine, something limited.

Through your spiritual practice you polish the lens that focusses the light that co-creates your experience. And as it is polished, the light can come through more and more purely, more and more in alignment with the divine pattern that already exists in higher dimensions of your Self, who you truly are. Your Earth body is just a shadow of a Higher Self. It is a reflection. And the light you are comes through that reflection. It comes through the reflected patterns of your beliefs, your ideas, your past experiences. And what you see on the screen, on the screen of the physical body and in the third and fourth dimensions of existence, is the playing out of those patterns. This is where the spiritual work is being done. Here is a planet on which this divine light has been misqualified. Many lesser patterns are afoot, lesser beliefs. Falsehoods have been reflected in this creation. In the higher dimensions all is in alignment. This world is where the action is. This is where the artistic achievement is being carried out. This is where the stone is being chipped away. This is where a planet is being re-created in its divine image. And those energies which have obstructed this divinity will be cast out. Their time is up! This is not a possibility — this is a promise! So I recommend to you, my dear friends, my dear brothers and sisters, that you have some gratitude for the experience that you are being offered in your life, the experience of knowing that there is a path to the real. Have some gratitude for the fact that you are here on this world now, in this moment, which is going to be so exciting and so wondrous to behold. In fact, there are many, many who would long to be also here with you in the physical. It is a blessing to be here now, to breathe, to know that you are well on your way home and that the energies of home do enfold you.

So, tonight I have a special treat for you, my friends. I hope you will enjoy it. It is what you call a guided meditation. I would like to call it a magical journey — so you don't think of it as work. Don't you get tired of hearing the word meditation? Don't you get tired of hearing your mind telling you that you should meditate more? Nag, nag, nag! Your mind will tell you that you are never doing it right, you know. Even if you are meditating, it will be certain to rear its head after you are finished and give you its commentary on the entire proceeding. "You are getting better. You are not as good as you used to be. You're totally lost. You're hopeless." Whatever the commentary might be. You see, that's the purpose of the mind, to give you feedback. But the more you enter that stillness within, the more you find peace and love overtaking you, as the commentary is replaced by a beautiful sense of joy and openness. You are where you are meant to be. And you can just open to that and enjoy what is before you. There is your canvas. What would you like to create on it? You can create whatever you like. You're the artists here.

So tonight, I would like to utilize your creative imaginations. With your permission, we will take a guided tour. I would like to begin it before your attention spans begin to waver.

So just relax. Take three or four deep breaths, all the way down into your bodies. Just relax yourselves. Loosen up if you have gotten stiff. I'm going to lead you on a guided journey. I know that some are more adept at following guided visualizations than others. I would like to assure you that you will benefit from this transmission, from this experience, regardless of your abilities to perfectly follow my directions. So you can tell that nagging mind to take off right now, and don't worry about doing it right. This is an artistic endeavor; that is, you just receive what comes and go with that.

So, I would like you to envision yourselves standing in a beautiful lane, with a beautiful green and rolling countryside all around you. Just stand for a moment and feel the Earth under your feet. Now visualize, off to your left, a smaller pathway leading to a stone gate, an arched stone gate. Walk up to the gate. You will see over the doorway some ancient figures or letters carved, ancient inscriptions. You feel called from within to enter this gate. And as you do, as you stand under the arch, beneath you, you see a beautiful paving stone, a large black polished obsidian stone under the archway. I ask you to simply walk up and stand upon it. And as you do, feel all tension drain from your body into the Earth. Feel your lower chakras opening and all tension draining, and feel your body becoming lighter.

As you do this, you open your eyes and see before you a beautiful stone tower, like a medieval castle. It is a round and tall tower with a pathway leading up to it, and you follow that path. Out of curiosity, with a sense of wonder, you approach the tower and you notice that winding around the outside of it is a spiral stairway. Now approach and begin to walk slowly up the stairs. As you walk, you notice ahead of you an area of dark red luminosity. You come to a platform on the stair and you see there, embedded in the stone wall of the tower, a dark red jewel or crystal. It is giving off a deep red light, very soothing, a very deep and healing energy. Take your left hand and place it on the stone, and place your right hand on your second chakra, just below your navel. Let the energy flow through into your second chakra, healing it, opening it, filling it with light and spiritual energy. And after a moment, when you feel complete, continue on up the stairs.

Walk up the spiral stair to the next level place, and there you see a yellow-orange colored light, and another jewel or crystal. Place your hand upon it and your other hand upon your third chakra, at your solar plexus, and absorb that healing energy. Let it flood through your third chakra. Let it cleanse all dense or heavy energies, filling your third chakra with light and healing energy. Just take a few deep breaths and allow this energy to enter you.

And then you continue on your journey up the stairs, winding around the tower. Climbing ever higher, you come to another flat platform on the stair, and see a beautiful pink rose-colored light flooding forth, and a beautiful rose-colored crystal or jewel. Again using your hands, absorb this healing energy into your heart chakra. Let that beautiful light enter your heart and open it. Let it fill you with love, pure unlimited love. Let it flood through your entire body from your heart all the way through your lower chakras and through your legs, and all the way upwards.

Just rest here a moment in this light.

Then you begin once again to climb the stairs, climbing higher up and around the tower. Now you come to another platform and a deep blue jewel or crystal giving off a pure blue light. Touch that with your left hand and place your right hand upon your throat chakra.

Just allow that energy to come through and open your throat chakra and align and balance the energy there, removing all tension. And when you are complete with this, go on up the stair.

Climb higher until you come to the last platform before the top of the tower. There you see an amethyst crystal emanating a beautiful violet light. Walk up to the wall and place your forehead right up against that crystal. Feel that beautiful light emanating through your body, opening your third eye, filling you with light. Just touch it to your brow and breathe. As you do, it opens your third eye, filling you with healing energy, flooding your entire body. Let this energy flow through you until you feel complete.

Finally you climb the last few steps to the top, to the roof of the tower. It is a flat round roof surrounded by a stone wall. There you see before you a beautifully carved stone chair and beside it a small pedestal. I ask you to sit in the chair. Just relax in the chair, and notice that on the pedestal there is a simple gold crown with four clear diamond crystals around it, completely pure and clear. I ask you to simply sit in the chair, and relax, and place the crown upon your head. Just sit and breathe. Feel the crown upon your head, and as you do, you feel your crown chakra like a thousand-petaled lotus, slowly opening. And as it opens, feel a stream of divine light coming from above in a column, coming down through your crown and into your body, flowing through all of your chakras. This light is gentle, yet powerful. Just sit for a moment and let that light enter you. As it flows through, it balances and opens all of your centers, purifies and transmutes any negative or dense energies, merging you with your divine Higher Self. Rest in this energy until you feel complete.

Now I ask you to allow the column of light to diminish in intensity as it rises back into the higher dimensions. Take the crown and place it back upon its spot on the pedestal. You will notice that the jewels are glowing much more brightly. And you will notice that your body and your being feel open and clear, at one with Spirit. When you are ready, perhaps, step down from your chair and walk around a bit on the tower. Look out over the walls at the kingdom blazing in etheric light, truly like the kingdom of heaven on Earth. And when you have had your view, seen what you have seen, I ask you to come back to the stairway and we will return the way we came.

As you begin the descent, there on your right side you feel once again the amethyst jewel. Touch it with your hand a moment in passing. As you do so it glows much more brightly, much more brilliantly, and you continue your descent. And do the same on the blue level. Touch the stone and it is recharged. And then slowly down through the fourth level where the rose jewel is shining. Touch it. Just allow it to recharge without diminishing your energy. See how it glows much more brightly. And continue down to the third level of the orange light, touching the stone in passing. Then down to the second level at the base of the stairway with the deep ruby red light, and just touch it in passing. Say farewell to your magical tower and walk once again down the path to the gate.

As you reach the gate, stand again upon the black stone. As you do so, you feel all of your chakras open and balanced. You feel the light of love coming down through your crown chakra, through all of your centers and into the Earth. And when you are complete with this, just walk out. As you do, your magical tower disappears. Now you see the stone gate and the inscription over the door. Perhaps you can read it now. If so, there is a message there for you. Then walk back down the path to the road and there just stand and allow your imagination to return you back to your seat here with me.

So, thank you for your focus, my dear princes and princesses of the kingdom of heaven. Just allow yourselves to come back into full body consciousness. Know that the energies that we have shared with you, the work that we have achieved, is permanently sealed and in effect, now and forever. So be it.

So my dear friends, my dear ones. I thank you this evening for your focus, for your attention, and for giving yourselves so wholeheartedly to our little mystery adventure. It took me some time to concoct that entire scenario for you. I hope you enjoyed it. I also am a master craftsman of sorts. As you go forth in your life, know that I am with you. Know that you can access these energies. You can perform this guided visualization on your own, if you wish. I will continue to assist you throughout your lives, throughout your endeavors. I will continue to be your muse in your artistic endeavors, inspiring you to go forward with love and compassion. I am yours. Goodnight.

About the Author

⇜ Eric Klein ⇝

Eric was initiated and began his spiritual path of meditation and service in 1972. He began conscious channeling of the Masters in 1986 with a period of inner instruction from many ascended teachers. In 1988, the first public channelings began with weekly evening gatherings, which then evolved into more specific classes and workshops under guidance from Sananda.

Eric continues to live in Santa Cruz, California, with his wife, Christine, who is also a channel (and an acupuncturist).

NOTE: To receive a catalog of Eric Klein's channeled tapes, send a self-addressed, stamped envelope to: Eric Klein Tapes, P.O. Box 498, Santa Cruz, CA 95061-0498 USA

ABOUT THE ARTIST

⋙ Cathie Beach ⋘

Cathie Beach is a clairvoyant healer and teacher who lives in Santa Cruz, California. She has been consciously combining her art and spirituality for more than eight years, and is becoming well known for her intuitive illustrations for book covers. Working with an author, she can create drawings which express the intent and feeling of the book in a unique way, and which will reach the intended audience.

Cathie also creates personalized, healing drawings. The images may be symbolic or abstract, and the colors resonate with the individual's energy system, giving support and balance. Many people are now using these drawings for gentle healing and personal empowerment.

Cathie feels her life is guided and blessed on a daily basis. She is committed to continuously stretch to be all that she can be, and to support others to do the same.

For additional information, please contact Oughten House Publications or write to Cathie Beach, P.O. Box 482, Soquel, CA 95073-0482.

ABOUT THE PUBLISHER AND LOGO

The name "Oughten" was revealed to the publisher fifteen years ago, after three weeks of meditation and contemplation. The combined effect of the letters carries a vibratory signature, signifying humanity's ascension on a planetary level.

The logo represents a new world rising from its former condition. The planet ascends from the darker to the lighter. Our experience of a dark and mysterious universe becomes transmuted by our planet's rising consciousness — glorious and spiritual. The grace of God transmutes the dross of the past into gold, as we leave all behind and ascend into the millennium.

PUBLISHER'S COMMENT

Our mission and purpose is to publish ascension books and complementary material for all peoples and all children worldwide.

We currently serve over fifty authors, musicians, and artists. Many of our authors channel such energies as Sananda, Ashtar, Archangel Michael, St. Germain, Archangel Ariel, Serapis, Mother Mary, and Kwan Yin. Some work closely with the Elohim and the angelic realms.They need your support to get their channeled messages to all nations. Oughten House Publications welcomes your interest and petitions your overall support and association in this important endeavor.

We urge you to share the information with your friends, and to join our network of spiritually-oriented people. Our financial proceeds are recycled into producing new ascension books and expanding our distribution worldwide. If you have the means to contribute or invest in this process, then please contact us.

OUGHTEN HOUSE PUBLICATIONS

Our imprint includes books in a variety of fields and disciplines which emphasize our relationship to the rising planetary consciousness. Literature which relates to the ascension process, personal growth, and our relationship to extraterrestrials is our primary focus. We are also developing a line of beautifully illustrated children's books, which deal with all aspects of spirituality. The list that follows is only a sample of our current offerings. To obtain a complete catalog, contact us at the address shown at the back of this book.

Ascension Books & Books for the Rising Planetary Consciousness

The Crystal Stair: A Guide to the Ascension, by Eric Klein. A collection of channeled teachings received from Lord Sananda (Jesus) and other Masters, describing the personal and planetary ascension process now actively occurring on our planet. — ISBN 1-880666-06-5, $12.95

The Inner Door: Channeled Discourses from the Ascended Masters on Self-Mastery and Ascension, by Eric Klein. In these two volumes, intended as a sequel to *The Crystal Stair*, the Masters address the challenges of the journey to ascension.

Volume One: ISBN 1-880666-03-0, $14.50
Volume Two: ISBN 1-880666-16-2, $14.50

Jewels on the Path: Transformational Teachings of the Ascended Masters, by Eric Klein. In this book, the ideas and themes introduced in Klein's earlier books are clarified and refined. The reader is brought up to date on what exactly the ascension process consists of and how to be a more active participant in it. Current topics are also discussed. This is the best one yet! —ISBN 1-880666-48-0, $14.95

An Ascension Handbook, by Tony Stubbs. A practical presentation which describes the ascension process in detail and includes several exercises to help you integrate it into your daily life. Topics include energy and matter; divine expression; love, power, and truth; breaking old patterns; aligning with Spirit; and life after ascension. A best-seller! — ISBN 1-880666-08-1, $12.95

What Is Lightbody? Archangel Ariel, channeled by Tashira Tachi-ren. Offers a twelve-level model for the ascension process, leading to the attainment of our Light Body. Recommended in *An Ascension Handbook*, this book gives many invocations, procedures, and potions to assist us on our journey home. Related tapes available. — ISBN 1-880666-25-1, $12.95

The Extraterrestrial Vision: Channeled Teachings from Theodore, channeled by Gina Lake. The mid-causal group entity, Theodore, tells us what we need to know about our extraterrestrial heritage and how to prepare for direct contact with those civilizations which will soon be appearing in our midst. — ISBN 1-880666-19-7, $13.50

Lady From Atlantis, by Robert V. Gerard. Shar Dae, the future empress of Atlantis, is suddenly transported onto a rain-soaked beach in modern-day America. There she meets her twin flame and discovers her mission: to warn the people of planet Earth to mend their ways before Mother Earth takes matters in her own hands! — ISBN 1-880666-21-9, $12.95

Intuition by Design, by Victor R. Beasley, Ph.D. A boxed set of 36 IQ (Intution Quotient) Cards contain conscious-ness-changing geometrics on one side and a transfomative verse on the other. The companion book tells you the many ways to use the cards in all aspects of your life. An incredible gift to yourself or someone you love. — ISBN 1-880666-22-7, $21.95

Navigating the '90s, by Deborah Soucek. Down-to-earth, practical ways to help yourself make the personal shifts in awareness and behavior required by these accelerated times. Loving and succinct observations and exercises through which we can reclaim our true selves and shed the "programming" of our past. ISBN 1-880666-28-X, $13.95 (available fourth quarter, 1995)

Angels of the Rays, by Mary Johanna. This book contains portraits of, information about, and messages from twelve different angels who are here to help us in our ascension process. Includes twelve removable full-color Angel Cards and directions for their use. — ISBN 1-880666-34-0, $18.95

My Ascension Journal, by Nicole Christine. Transform yourself and your life by using the journaling methods given in this book. Includes several real-life examples from the author's own journals, plus many blank pages on which to write your own ascension story. This quality-bound edition will become a treasured keepsake to be re-read over and over again. — ISBN 1-880666-18-9, $24.95 (available fourth quarter, 1995)

Bridge Into Light: Your Connection to Spiritual Guidance, by Pam and Fred Cameron. Lovingly offers many step-by-step exercises on how to meditate and how to channel, and gives ways to invoke the protection and assistance of the Masters. Companion tape available. — ISBN 1-880666-07-3, $11.95

Transformational Tools

We offer an ever-expanding selection of transformational tools to assist you in your journey back to mastery. These include books and tapes, with such titles as *Intuition by Design, Heart Initiation, Ascending From the Center, Ascension: Beginner's Manual, The Thymus Chakra Handbook, Parallel Realities, The Feminine Aspect of God,*

Ascension Merkabah, Soul Alignment, Joshua Stone's books on ascension, and several series of tapes by authors such as Tashira Tachi-ren, Solara, August Stahr, and Crea. Hear the voices and experience the energies of our authors, on companion tapes to *Bridge Into Light* and *The Extraterrestrial Vision*.We also have products such as Ascension Cards to help you focus on your ascension process as it unfolds in your life. For more information on these and other titles in this category, please call or write for our free catalog.

Children's Books and Tapes

Books and tapes in this category include titles such as *Nature Walk, Mary's Lullaby, Song of Gothar, Bear Essentials of Love*, and the "Little Angel" book series. Although primarily intended for children and adults who interact with children, they speak to the "child" within us all.

Music Tapes

We carry many titles of spiritually-based music, including both vocal and instrumental types, by artists such as Richard Shulman, Omashar, Stefan Jedland, and Michael Hammer. Create your own "ascension chamber" whenever you play them — at home or wherever your journey takes you. For a listing of available titles, call or write for our free catalog. A reply card is bound into this book for your convenience, or you may reach us at the location listed on the back page.

ATTENTION: BUSINESSES AND SCHOOLS!

OUGHTEN HOUSE books are available at quantity discounts with bulk purchases for educational, business, or sales promotional use. For details, please contact the publisher at the address on page 239.

READER NETWORKING AND MAILING LIST

The ascension process presents itself as a new reality for many of us on planet Earth. Many Starseeds and Light-workers seek to know more. Thousands of people worldwide are reaching out to find others of like mind and to network with them. The newly formed Oughten House Foundation stands ready to serve you all.

You have the opportunity to become a member, stay informed, and be on our networking mailing list. Send us the enclosed Information Reply Card or a letter. We will do our best to keep you and your network of friends up to date with ascension-related literature, materials, author tours, workshops, and channelings.

NOTE: If you have a network database or small mailing list you would like to share, please send it along!

 Announcing ...

Oughten House Foundation, Inc. has recently been created as a publishing, educational, and networking organization. The purpose of the Foundation is to serve all those who seek personal, social, and spiritual empowerment. Our goal is to reach out to 560 million people worldwide. The Foundation has a non-profit (501 (c),(d)) status and seeks members and other fund-raising affiliations. Programs for all age groups will be offered.

An integral part of our mission involves the development of a global network to support the dissemination of information, especially through organized community groups. Information related to membership and program services is available upon request. Please contact Oughten House Publications, or call (510) 447-2332.

CATALOG REQUESTS & BOOK ORDERS

Catalogs will gladly be sent upon request. For catalogs to be sent outside of the USA, please send $3.00 for postage and handling. Book orders must be prepaid: check, money order, international coupon, VISA, MasterCard, Discover Card, and American Express accepted. Include UPS shipping and handling as follows (no P.O. boxes for UPS):

UPS Domestic Shipping and Handling:

ORDER TOTAL			GROUND	3-DAY	2-DAY	NEXT DAY
$00.01	to	$10.00	$ 4.50	$ 6.00	$ 8.25	$16.00
$10.01	to	$30.00	$ 5.75	$ 7.25	$10.00	$19.50
$30.01	to	$50.00	$ 7.00	$ 8.25	$11.25	$21.00
$50.01	to	$70.00	$ 8.50	$10.25	$12.50	$25.00
$70.01	to	$100.00	$10.50	$13.00	$14.50	$27.50
$100.01	to	$150.00*	$12.50	$15.75	$17.50	$35.00

*All orders over $150.00 need to call for a shipping estimate
*HI, AK, PR orders are shipped Priority Mail or Book Rate
*All continental US orders shipped UPS unless requested otherwise

*Allow 48 hours to process all regular orders

INTERNATIONAL ORDERS:

Charges include actual shipping costs for international Air or Surface Printed Matter, plus an additional $4.00 handling fee.

If paying by check or money order, please use US funds, through a US bank or an International Money Order, payable to Oughten House Publications. Allow approximately 6 weeks for international delivery and 10 working days for US delivery. (Note: Book prices, shipping, and handling charges are subject to change.)
To place your order, call, fax, or mail to:

OUGHTEN HOUSE PUBLICATIONS
P.O. Box 2008
Livermore • California • 94551-2008 • USA
Phone (510) 447-2332
Fax (510) 447-2376

Oughten House Information/Order Card

□ Send me your free catalog
(For international catalog requests, send $3.00 S & H)

□ Please send me ____ sets of Ascension Cards
at $12.95 each plus S & H (see below)

□ Please send me information on the benefits of becoming a member of Oughten House Foundation, Inc.

□ Please send me the following publications:

Qty.	Book Title	US Retail Price	Total
	The Crystal Stair, by Eric Klein	$12.95	
	The Inner Door, by Eric Klein □ Vol. I □ Vol. II	(@ $14.50 each)	
	Jewels on the Path, by Eric Klein	$14.95	
	An Ascension Handbook, by Tony Stubbs	$12.95	
	What Is Lightbody? Archangel Ariel, channeled by Tashira Tachi-ren	$12.95	
	Bridge Into Light, by Pam and Fred Cameron	$11.95	
	The Extraterrestrial Vision: Channeled Teachings from Theodore, by Gina Lake	$13.50	
	Navigating the '90s, by Deborah Soucek	$13.95	
	Angels of the Rays (book + 12 Angel Cards)	$18.95	
	Intuition By Design (book + 36 IQ Cards), by Dr. Victor Beasley	$21.95	
	Lady From Atlantis, by Robert V. Gerard	$12.95	
		S & H	
	California residents add 8.25% tax.	Tax	
	Make checks payable to Oughten House. TOTAL ENCLOSED (US Funds, please**) $		

Shipping: $4.50 + $1.50 each additional item (please add $3.00 to international orders)

Master Card, Visa, Discover, American Express:* Account # _ _ _ _ _ _ _ _ _ _ _ _ _ _ _ Exp. Date _ _ /199 _

**International customers: US funds drawn on US bank / International Money Order; extra shipping may apply.

Signature _____

Name _____

Address _____

City _____ State/Province _____ Zip _____

Country _____ Home Phone (___) _____

*Please Note: For credit card purchases, we recommend that you send this order card to us, enclosed in an envelope to protect your credit card number, **or call (510) 447-2232** to place your order.

BRC:4Q/95

From:

_____

_____

_____

_____

"*Books and Tools for the Rising Planetary Consciousness*"

OUGHTEN HOUSE PUBLICATIONS

P.O. Box 2008

Livermore, CA 94551-2008

USA

Affix a
32¢ Stamp